Steps to Christ

To God,
for fighting for our recovery.
How cool is He!

Steps to Christ
RECOVERY EDITION

Cheri Peters
with Sophie Berecz

True Step Ministries
PO Box 163, Kuna, Idaho
www.truestep.org

PO Box 220, West Frankfort, Illinois
www.3ABN.org

Cheri Peters is the founder of True Step Ministries
Sophie Berecz is a freelance writer in Boise, Idaho

True Step Ministries, Inc., Kuna, ID

Editor: Fran McKain
Book design: Fran McKain
Photo credits-Cover: © Masterpiece Studio

Steps to Christ, Recovery Edition is an adaptation of the original *Steps to Christ* by Ellen White. It was adapted for True Step Ministries and those they serve. The entire book has been updated to recovery language and integrated with the well-known 12 steps of recovery, but the message remains the same. All Bible quotes are from the New Living Translation.

Published 2013 by True Step Ministries, Inc. and 3ABN Books

3ABN Books is dedicated to bringing you the best in published materials consistent with the mission of Three Angels Broadcasting Network. Our goal is to uplift Jesus through books, audio, and video materials by our family of 3ABN presenters. Our in-depth Bible study guides, devotionals, biographies, and lifestyle materials promote the whole person in health and the mending of broken people. For more information, call 618-627-4651 or visit 3ABN's Web site: http://www.3ABN.org

ISBN (paperback): 978-1-4675-7614-7

Contents

S T E P 1

We admitted we were powerless over our addictions and compulsive behaviors, that our lives had become unmanageable.

"I know that nothing good lives in me, that is, in my sinful nature. For I have the desire to do what is good, but I cannot carry it out."

~ Romans 7:18

CHAPTER 1

God is Crazy About You!
(God's Love for Man)

When you hit rock bottom, you'll discover that you are deeply loved.

God is crazy about you! Like a star-struck lover, He writes love messages everywhere. Life and everything good pour out from Him like a love song. Stop and look around you. Do you see how He designed everything in nature to perfectly meet our needs? That didn't happen by accident. It's not just survival of the fittest. The sun and rain that refresh the earth, the mountains and valleys and seas and stars all remind us of our Creator's love. God provides everything we need every day. The Bible says, "All eyes look to you for help; you give them their food as they need it. When you open your hand, you satisfy the hunger and thirst of every living thing" (Psalm 145:15,16).

Love's Many Voices

God made Adam and Eve perfect and happy, and the earth, when He first made it, was perfect too. There was no sickness or death, no addictions or dysfunction. It wasn't until they disobeyed God's law—the law of love—that trouble and death began. The foundation of love and trust cracked, and aftershocks of misery have struck every one of us. But even in our pain, God is still taking care of us. The Bible says God cursed the ground for our good (Genesis 3:17). The thorns and thistles—those hard times that make life such a grind—actually help us. They loosen our grip on the things that hurt us and bring us shame. They help us to see that we're powerless over our addictions and compulsive behaviors—that our lives have become unmanageable. The hard times open our hearts to His plan to lift us out of the mess we've made of our lives.

The beauty of nature gives us encouraging glimpses of God's rescue plan. This world, as awful as it can be, is not all pain and misery. Flowers bloom on the thistles, and roses cover the thorns. Every beautiful flower and every blade of grass sends the message "God is love, and He is crazy about you!" The sweet songs of the birds, the delicate colors and fragrances of flowers, the towering trees of the forest— all tell of our Father's care and how much He longs to make His children happy and to reconnect them to Himself.

The Bible, also, shows us God's character. It's a message directly from Him to say, "I have adored you forever, and I always will. I care about everything that touches you." When Moses prayed, "Please let me see the wonder of You," God answered, "I will make all my goodness pass before you" (Exodus 33:18,19). His goodness is what makes Him so amazing. God told Moses, "I am the Lord, I am the Lord, the merciful and gracious God. I am slow to anger and rich in unfailing love and faithfulness. I show this unfailing love to many thousands by forgiving every kind of sin and rebellion" (Exodus 34:6,7). He is "slow to get angry and filled with unfailing love" (Jonah 4:2), "because He delights in showing mercy" (Micah 7:18).

God draws our hearts to Him in a million different ways. Through the wonders of nature and the deepest and most tender human relationships, He gives us glimpses of His heart. These are only imperfect hints—only a small taste of His vast love. And the tragedy is that despite the torrent of love behind these beautiful gifts, God's enemy, Satan, confuses our minds so we misunderstand God's heart. Sadly, many people are afraid of God and think He's cold and unforgiving. Satan wants us to see God as a cruel, demanding judge who is waiting to catch us making mistakes so He can condemn us. That's why Jesus stepped into this world to show us God's love—a deeper love than any we've ever known or could possibly imagine. God loves us more than life itself and He delights to forgive us and heal us.

Jesus-the Face of the Father's Love

Jesus, the Son of God, came from heaven to show us what our Father is really like. "No one has ever seen God. But his only Son, who is himself God, is near to the Father's heart; he has told us about him" (John 1:18). "No one really knows the Son except the Father, and no one really knows the Father except the Son and those to whom the Son chooses to reveal him" (Matthew 11:27). When one of His followers asked, "Show us the Father," Jesus answered, "don't you even yet know who I am, even after all the time I have been with you? Anyone who has seen Me has seen the Father!" (John 14:8,9).

Jesus said that God had sent Him "to preach Good News to the poor. He has sent me to proclaim that captives will be released, that the blind will see, that the downtrodden will be freed from their oppressors" (Luke 4:18). That was His work. Everywhere Jesus went He helped people and healed the victims of Satan's abuse. There were whole towns where not one person was sick after Jesus came because He had healed them all. The compassion of God showed in everything Jesus did; His heart reached out in tender love to everyone. Jesus became a human just like us so He could connect with us and help us. The outcasts, who everyone else rejected, were not afraid to come near Him. Even little children were drawn to Him; they loved to climb into His lap and gaze into His kind and gentle face.

Jesus always spoke kindly, even when He told someone a difficult truth. He listened thoughtfully and gave each person His full attention when He talked with them. He was never rude; He never spoke harshly; and He never hurt anyone. Jesus didn't criticize people for being weak or for having faults. Instead, He told them the truth with love. Even when Jesus spoke against hypocrisy, unbelief, and evil, there were tears in His voice. Jesus cried over Jerusalem, the city He loved. His heart broke for the people who had refused to receive Him, the one who was the Way, the Truth, and the Life. They had rejected Him, even though He was the only one who could save them from their dysfunctions and addictions. But despite their rejection, He still cared deeply about them. He always looked out for others even when it meant personal loss for Himself. Every person was important to Him. Even though He was the Son of God, Jesus was never too good for anyone. He took special interest in the life of every person He met, no matter how little they mattered to anyone else. In every wounded person He saw friend that He had come to save.

Jesus' life showed us exactly what God is like. Through Jesus, we see God's great compassion for each of us. Jesus, the kind and caring Savior, was God "in the flesh" (1 Timothy 3:16)—God with skin on.

Jesus lived and suffered and died to save us. He became "a Man of sorrows" so we can escape the grief of our lives on this earth and have lives of joy. God adores His Son, but He let Jesus leave heaven, a place of incredible joy and love, to come to a world cursed by sin and death. Jesus left His place beside the Father, He left the angels who adored Him, to come down here and suffer shame, insult, hate, and death. "He was beaten that we might have peace. He was whipped, and we were healed" (Isaiah 53:5). Picture in your mind the suffering of Jesus in the wilderness, His agony in the garden of Gethsemane, and the torture when He was nailed on the cross! The sinless Son of God took on Himself the guilty stain and terrible burden of our sins. Though Jesus had been united with God in heaven, He now felt the awful separation that sin brings between God and us. His tormented heart cried out, "My God, my God, why have you forsaken me?" (Matthew 27:46). It was the crushing guilt of our sin that ripped Jesus away from God and broke His heart.

The Father Who Delights in Our Recovery

Did Jesus die to convince the Father to save us? Absolutely not! It was the Father who sent Him, and God sent Jesus because He's crazy about us. Jesus said, "The Father loves me because I lay down my life that I may have it back again" (John 10:17). He wanted us to know that the Father loves us just as much as He does. In fact, "God so loved the world that He gave His only Son" (John 3:16). The Father gave Jesus to us because He can't bear to lose us.

Through Jesus, God poured out His relentless love upon a bruised and broken world. "God was in Christ, reconciling the world to Himself" (2 Corinthians 5:19). God suffered with His Son. In the agony of Jesus' suffering and His awful death on the cross, God paid the price of our full recovery.

Only the Son of God could save us, because only He was close enough to the Father's heart to be able to show us God's passionate love. Nothing less than the enormous sacrifice Jesus made for sinners could give us a clear picture of the Father's vast love for us.

"God so loved the world that He gave His only Son" (John 3:16). He gave Him not only to live among us, to take responsibility for our sins, and to die our death; but God literally gave Jesus to us. Jesus became a human just like us. How else could He know our longings and needs? Jesus, who was united with God, became eternally united with us. Jesus is "not ashamed to call [us] his brothers and sisters" (Hebrews 2:11); He is our sacrifice, our attorney, our brother, standing as a human before the Father's throne, continually there to help us. Through eternity, Jesus, the "Son of Man," will keep His humanity. He now belongs to those He saved. That was the price God paid to rescue us from the ruin and shame of sin and to reconnect us with Himself and with each other. How amazing is that!

When you stop to think of the price paid to rescue us—the infinite price our Father paid in giving Jesus to die for us—you can begin to imagine all He has in store for our lives. John struggled to find words to express the Father's great love toward our dying race. Finally he just called us to look and see "how very much our heavenly Father loves us, for he allows us to be called his children, and we really are!" (1 John 3:1). We're priceless to Him! Through disobedience we became slaves of Satan. But through Jesus' death we can become God's own children. By taking on our human nature and becoming one of us, Jesus raised us up to become like Him—to become part of the Father's family and to bear the family name.

Where else can we find such a love as this? We're children of the heavenly King. What a promise! Nothing compares to the love of God towards a world that does not love Him back. The more we think about what God has done for us, the more willing we become to follow His plan for our lives. The more we learn about God's character and what He did for us at the cross, the more we understand His tenderness and forgiveness as well as His fairness and justice. The more clearly we see that God is crazy about us, the more we'll trust that He takes deep joy in our recovery and that He can restore us to sanity. Be amazed at the Father's kindness and concern for us, which is deeper than even a mother's yearning love for a rebellious child!

Discussion Questions

1. What do you think God is like? What influenced your perception of Him?

2. Studies have shown that our "God concept" is formed by the authority figures in our lives—especially our fathers. Their beliefs, attitudes and actions and the way they treated us affect our view of God. We tend to either think God is like them or we see Him in the same way they do.

    What connection do you see between the way you were taught or treated by the authority figures in your life and the way you view God?

3. What do you see in nature that suggest God cares about us?

4. Who is the most caring person you know? What does that person do that makes you feel loved?

5. While nature and human relationships give hints about God's love, they don't give a clear picture. They are damaged by sin. Before sin, there was no ugliness, addiction or brokenness. There was no sickness, violence, or death in nature. There was no selfishness, abuse, or hate in human relationships. Everywhere the love of the Creator was obvious. Not now.

    How did that happen?

    Genesis 1:26, 27 _____

    Revelation 12:7-9 _____

    Isaiah 14:12-15 _____

Genesis 3:1-19 _____

Romans 8:19-21 _____

Deuteronomy 32:5 _____

6. What are some ways God has communicated with people to help us see His love more clearly?

Genesis 15:1; Psalm 102:18-19; Jeremiah 30:1-2

What was the best way God showed us that He loves us?
Luke 4:18; John 3:16; John 6:37-40; 1 John 4:9-10

7. In the Bible are stories where God cries out from his heart to us because He loves us so much and wants so much to heal our brokenness and pain. Consider the verse below as just one example.

> *I've loved you since you were a child. I called you, but you turned away from me. Still, I kept teaching you, guiding you, comforting you, healing you, but you didn't even know it was me! I drew you to me with cords of love, bending down to you and gently feeding you. But you refused to turn to me even though you kept being wounded. How can I give you up?! How can I surrender you or send you away? How can I let you be destroyed? My heart recoils within me. My compassion is on fire for you. I will not let you be destroyed! I am crying out, roaring like a lion, calling my children to return to me!*
> *~ Hosea 11:1-10 (paraphrase)*

How does your heart respond to this picture of God?

S T **2** E P

We came to believe that a power greater than ourselves could restore us to sanity.

"For it is God who works in you to will and to act according to His good purpose."

~ *Philippians 2:13*

CHAPTER 2

Help! I Need Jesus

(The Sinner's Need of Christ)

If you're lost in your junk, know that God delights in your recovery!

In the beginning, Adam and Eve were strong and perfect in mind and body. They adored God and only wanted to please Him. But after they believed Satan's lies and disobeyed God, their minds were twisted. Instead of loving God, they cared only about themselves. That one act of disobedience crippled them and they became powerless over their behavior. Their lives became unmanageable. Satan easily took advantage of them and trapped them like slaves in a life of dysfunction and misery.

Every person since has been born enslaved. Satan intended to fill the earth with grief and pain and then point to all this evil and say it was God's fault since He had created us. All humanity would have remained his victims forever if God had not stepped in to rescue us.

Unmanageable and Powerless

Before Adam sinned, he loved to talk with God. Think what it was like to talk with the One who is the source of all wisdom and knowledge (Colossians 2:3)! But when he rebelled, Adam disconnected from God. He became afraid and wanted to hide. It's like that for all of us until God changes our hearts. We get disconnected from God and caught up in our dysfunction and addictions, and we can't enjoy talking with Him. As sinners, we could never be happy being with God or with those who love Him. If God let us into heaven we'd hate it. We would never understand the unselfish motives of the angels. Because of our evil thoughts and interests, we'd feel like misfits. We'd be like a wrong note, out-of-tune with the melody of heaven. Heaven would actually be torture to us. We would want to run away and hide from God—the One who is the source of joy to everyone else. That's why God leaves it up to us to choose whether we want to be with Him in heaven or not. He won't force us to be with Him because, as sinners, His holiness and glory would consume us like fire. In our sin, we'd welcome death in order to hide from Jesus, the One who died to save us.

It is impossible for you, on your own, to escape from sin. As a descendant of Adam, your nature is evil and you can't change it. "Who can create purity in one born impure? No one!" (Job 14:4); "For the sinful nature is always hostile to God. It never did obey God's laws, and it never will" (Romans 8:7). Education, culture, the exercise of your will power, and your own effort all have their proper place, but when it comes to saving you from sin, they are powerless. These things may help you to behave correctly, but they can't change your nature; they can't make you clean inside. There is only one power that can get rid of your sin and begin a new and holy life in you. That power is Jesus. Only His grace can bring life to your lifeless soul and make you want to be with God and be holy.

Jesus said, "I tell you the truth, unless you are born again," unless you receive a new heart, new desires, new purposes and motives, leading to a new life, "you cannot see the Kingdom of God" (John 3:3). The idea that you just need to develop your own natural goodness in order to overcome sin is a dangerous lie. "People who aren't spiritual can't receive these truths from God's Spirit. It all sounds foolish to them and they can't understand it, for only those who are spiritual can understand what the Spirit means" (1 Corinthians 2:14). That's why Jesus said, "don't be surprised when I say, 'You must be born again'" (John 3:7). The Bible says Jesus "gave life to everything that was created, and his life brought light to everyone" (John 1:4). Jesus' name is the only "name under heaven by which we must be saved" (Acts 4:12).

It's not enough to see the kindness and generosity of God and to accept that He's a caring Father. It's not enough to recognize the wisdom and fairness of His law and to see that it's based on love. The apostle Paul saw all of that when he said, "I agree that the law is good." "The law itself is holy, and its commands are holy and right and good." But he added, in the bitterness of anguish and despair, "I am all too human, a slave to sin" (Romans 7:16,12,14). Paul ached to be pure inside, but no matter how hard he tried, he couldn't change. In deep torment, he cried out, "Oh, what a miserable person I am! Who will free me from this life that is dominated by sin and death?" (Romans 7:24). Many people throughout history have echoed his cry. And there is only one answer, "Look! The Lamb of God who takes away the sin of the world!" (John 1:29).

The One Who Can Restore Us to Sanity

How many stories, how many examples has the Holy Spirit used to help us understand this truth! He tries every way possible to show us the One who can free us from our burden of guilt. The Bible tells the story of Jacob who took advantage of his brother, Esau, and ran away to save his own skin. He felt like a lonely outcast, guilty and ashamed and separated from everything that made his life worth living. But one thought tortured him most of all: He was afraid that his sin had cut him off from God forever. In misery, he lay down to sleep on the ground, surrounded by the lonely hills and the night sky above. As he slept, Jacob saw a strange light. From where he lay on the ground, huge shadowy stairs seemed to reach to the very gates of heaven, and on the stairs he saw angels climbing up and down. From the glory above, he heard God's voice, and it filled him with comfort and hope. Jacob had been shown what he so desperately needed—he had been shown a Savior. He must have cried with joy and gratitude to see how he, a sinner, could be reconnected to God. The ladder he saw in his dream represented Jesus who makes it possible for us to communicate with God.

Jesus, also, talked about the ladder when He was here on earth. He told Nathaniel, "you will all see heaven open and the angels of God going up and down on the Son of Man," the Son who is the stairway between heaven and earth (John 1:51). In the rebellion, Adam tore the whole human race away from God; earth was cut off from heaven. Across the gulf that lay between, there could be no communication. But Jesus linked earth with heaven again. His perfect life bridged the gap sin had caused. Jesus connects ruined people, in all their weakness and helplessness, with the Source of infinite power.

Without the power of God, all our hopes for recovery, all our efforts at self-improvement are pointless. "Whatever is good and perfect comes down to us from God" (James 1:17). No one can have a truly good character without God. And the only way to God is through Jesus. Jesus says, "I am the way, the truth, and the life. No one can come to the Father except through Me" (John 14:6).

God's heart yearns over His earthly children with a love that is stronger than death. When He gave us His Son, God poured out all the resources of heaven in one gift. All of heaven works together to bring us to full recovery: Jesus lived and died and intervenes for us, the angels help us, the Spirit pleads for us, and the Father works above all and through all to restore us to wholeness and holiness.

What an amazing sacrifice God made for us! Imagine the intense effort and energy God uses to bring us back to Himself. What stronger forces or greater incentives could He possibly use? The incredible rewards for doing what's right, the thrill and joy of heaven, the privilege of learning and growing forever, the friendship of the angels, the intimate connection with God and His Son who love us so deeply—aren't these reasons enough for us to give our hearts in loving service to our Creator and Rescuer? And, on the other hand, there are the terrible warnings in the Bible about the inescapable consequences for those who serve Satan: God's judgments against sin, the corruption of the character, and final destruction.

Think about God's kindness and patience! What more could He do? How can we not run back into the arms of God who loves us with such amazing love? Let's return to the One who longs for our recovery so He can restore us and we can be with Him forever.

Discussion Questions

1. Why is it not enough to notice the love and kindness of God? Deuteronomy 32:5; Isaiah 53:6; Ezekiel 18:20; Romans 6:23.

2. The Bible speaks of being trapped by sin in a body of death (Romans 7:24). Do you consider yourself helpless on your own to change the brokenness inside you? How did you finally come to recognize that?

3. The Bible says death is the result of sin (Romans 6:23). Why must this be?

4. If someone you love cheated on you and got AIDS, you couldn't save their life by just forgiving them, right? To save their life, you would have to get rid of the infection. Sin is like that. What does it take to get rid of the sin inside us? Matthew 26:28; Romans 5:8-10; 1 John 1:7-9.

5. God loves you so much He would rather die than give you up. At this point in your life, how do you want to respond to that?

S T 3 E P

We made a decision to turn our wills and our lives over to the care of God.

"Therefore, I urge you, brothers, in view of God's mercy, to offer your bodies as living sacrifices, holy and pleasing to God – this is your spiritual act of worship."
~ Romans 12:1

CHAPTER 3

Sorry Enough to Quit

(God's Love for Man)

When you hit rock bottom, you'll discover that you are deeply loved.

D o you wonder how you can ever be clean and right with God—how you can ever have peace with Him and become pure inside? You've come to realize that you're powerless over your addictions and compulsive behaviors and that only Jesus can restore you to sanity. But how can you come to Jesus? How can you turn your life over to Him? Maybe you're crying out, "What should I do?" The answer is simple, "Repent of your sins and turn to God, so that your sins may be wiped away" (Acts 3:19).

False Repentance

Repentance means being sorry for sin—sorry enough to quit. You won't turn away from sin unless you see how wrong it is. Your life won't really change until you turn away from sin in your heart. It's not enough to be sorry you made bad choices, especially not if your real motive is the fear of being caught or of suffering the consequences of your choices. That's not repentance as God sees it.

The Bible has many stories of people who "repented" this way. There's Esau, the firstborn son of Isaac, who foolishly traded off his position as the spiritual leader of his family. When he discovered that he'd also given up his inheritance, his only real regret was the monetary loss. And there's Balaam who was terrified when a sword-wielding angel confronted him while he was doing the very thing God had forbidden. He confessed his guilt in order to save his life, but he didn't really regret what he was doing. He still wanted to do it. He felt no disgust over the evil in his heart.

Judas Iscariot was the man who betrayed Jesus. After the authorities bought him off, he regretted what he'd done and cried out, "I have sinned for I have betrayed an innocent man" (Matthew 27:4)! The awful shame and fear of the consequences forced this confession from his guilty soul. Judas was terrified of his own fate, but he had no deep, heartbroken grief that he had betrayed the sinless Son of God. Pharaoh defied God until Egypt was destroyed. When he finally admitted his rebellion it was only to escape further punishment. He rebelled again as soon as the plagues stopped. All of these people regretted the results of their sin, but they were not really sorry for having committed the sin itself.

Real Repentance

Real repentance is not like that at all. When God's Spirit touches your heart, you'll have a clear sense of right and wrong. You'll deeply respect God's holy law which is the foundation of His government. Jesus, the "true Light, who gives light to everyone," will shine a light on all the

sins you have tried to keep secret (John 1:9). The con-
viction of right and wrong will take hold on your heart.
You'll see the great holiness of God and feel the terror of
standing before Him in your guilt, fully exposed to the
One who sees everything. But when you see how much He
loves you in spite of your shame, you'll long for Him to
cleanse you and you'll want to be close to Him.

King David's prayer gives us an example of true grief
for sin. He had committed both adultery and murder.
David saw the awfulness of his sin. He saw the corruption in his heart, and he despised it. His repentance was
intense. David didn't try to hide his guilt. He didn't try
to escape the consequences. He prayed not just to be forgiven, but also for a clean heart. He longed to reconnect
with God. He said:

"Oh, what joy for those whose rebellion is forgiven,
whose sin is put out of sight! Yes, what joy for those whose
record the LORD has cleared of sin, whose lives are lived
in complete honesty" (Psalm 32:1,2)! "Have mercy on me,
O God, because of your unfailing love. Because of your
great compassion, blot out the stain of my sins. For I recognize my shameful deeds—they haunt me day and night.
Purify me from my sins, and I will be clean; wash me, and
I will be whiter than snow. Create in me a clean heart, O
God. Renew a right spirit within me. Do not banish me
from your presence, and don't take your Holy Spirit from
me. Restore to me again the joy of your salvation, and
make me willing to obey you. Forgive me for shedding
blood, O God who saves; then I will joyfully sing of your
forgiveness" (Psalm 51:1,3,7,10-12,14).

In your own power, you can't repent like that. Such a
deep change of heart comes only as a gift from Jesus—the
One who overcame sin for us.

You Can't Do It On Your Own

Don't miss this point! Don't miss out on the help Jesus wants to give you. If you think you can't come to Him until you're sorry for your sins, please know that isn't how it works. It's true that repentance comes before forgiveness because it's only when your heart is broken over your sin that you'll feel your need of a Savior. But do you have to wait until you feel sorry before you can come to Him? Is repentance a roadblock between you and Jesus?

The Bible does not teach that! It doesn't say you must be sorry for your sins before you can accept Jesus' invitation, "Come to me, all of you who are weary and carry heavy burdens, and I will give you rest" (Matthew 11:28). It's the goodness of Jesus that leads us to repent. Peter made this very clear when he said God sent Jesus to give us both repentance and forgiveness (Acts 5:31). Jesus changes how you see your addictions and your sins. He brings you to a heartfelt regret for the damage your mistakes have caused to yourself and others. At the same time He forgives you.Not only does Jesus help you to see the full picture of the damage your sin has caused, He changes your desires, giving you a hatred for sin and a desire to do what's right. Every time you clearly see your sin, every time you want to be pure, you can be sure His Spirit is working on your heart.

Jesus said, "When I am lifted up from the earth, I will draw everyone to myself" (John 12:32). Think about Jesus dying for the sins of the entire world and you'll begin to understand God's incredible plan to save us. It's God's goodness that leads us to repent. How do you even get your head around the idea of someone who would die for a world in rebellion? The very thought will bring you to your knees in love and repentance.

It's true people sometimes become ashamed and stop doing the wrong thing before they even know Jesus is working in them. But whenever you sincerely try to do right, it's because Jesus is touching your heart. You may have no idea His Holy Spirit is at work, but gradually you'll become aware of right and wrong and your actions and habits will change. When you see it was your sin that sent Jesus to the cross, you'll recognize the importance of God's law. You'll see the deep-seated sin in your life. You'll understand something of God's great goodness and fairness, and in amazement you'll say, "How awful is sin that it caused the death of God! Was all this love, all this suffering and shame, necessary, so I can live and not die?"

You can resist His love. You can refuse to be drawn to Him. But why would you want to, when you realize that He's been working to rescue you since long before time began? Knowing that, you'll fall at the foot of the cross, filled with sorrow for the suffering your sin has caused Him.

God is speaking to your heart, creating a craving you can't explain for something you don't have. Addictions, sinful pleasure, money: these things can never satisfy your longing. The Spirit of God is pleading with you to come to Jesus—the only One who can truly satisfy your thirst. He's doing everything possible to make you want His good ways instead of the things that will destroy you. Don't keep trying to drink from the broken water-fountains of this world. God says, "Let anyone who is thirsty come. Let anyone who desires drink freely from the water of life" (Revelation 22:17).

If you long for something better than this world can give, recognize this longing as God's voice speaking to your soul. Ask Him to give you repentance. Ask Him to help you really see Jesus-the perfect example of what it means to love God and love people. His life was all kindness and unselfish love. As you look at Jesus you'll clearly see the contrast between His goodness and your sin.

The Love That Reveals

You may have thought that your life has been good, that you haven't done anything really bad. You may tell yourself, "I'm not a drug addict or a thief." You may think you don't need to humble your heart before God like other sinners. But when the light of Jesus shines into your soul, you'll see how messed up you really are; you'll recognize your selfish motives and the bitterness and hatred against God that have tainted your actions. Then you'll know that you have no goodness of your own; that only the blood of Jesus can cleanse you from the shame and filth of sin. Only Jesus can renew your mind to be like His.

You only need to catch a little glimpse of the love and purity of God to see, by contrast, the twisted brokenness of your own heart. Jesus will pull away the mask so you can see your warped desires and the corruption and treachery inside. God will expose your rebellion against Him and your refusal to obey His law of love. His Holy Spirit will convict you. When you see the pure and perfect character of Jesus you'll grieve over the sin that lurks inside your heart.

When the prophet Daniel saw the glory of the angel who came to him, he was overwhelmed with a sense of his own weakness and imperfection. He said, "My strength left me, my face grew deathly pale, and I felt very weak" (Daniel 10:8). When your life is touched by God, you'll hate your selfishness and self-love. You'll ask God for a clean heart that willingly obeys Him and that reflects the character of Jesus.

Paul said he looked perfect on the outside (Philippians 3:6); but when he realized God's law requires far more than correct behavior he knew he was in trouble. He had avoided all the outward mistakes and obvious sins. But when he looked deeper into the perfect, holy law of God, Paul saw himself as God saw him, and he bowed in shame and confessed his guilt. Paul said, "I lived without understanding the law. But when I learned the command not to covet, for instance, the power of sin came to life" (Romans 7:9). When Paul saw that God's law called him to love others, he realized how corrupt his heart was inside and he repented of his arrogance.

All Sins Are Not Equal

God does not view all sins as being equal; like us, God sees sin in varying degrees of guilt; but however trivial it seems to us, no sin is small in the sight of God. Our view is clouded and incomplete, but God see things as they really are. Some people despise alcoholics and addicts and tell them their sin will keep them out of heaven. Those same people often think nothing of pride, selfishness, and jealously. But to God, these sins are even worse because they are directly contrary to the kindness and thoughtfulness of His character. That kind of attitude doesn't exist in heaven. The person who does things that are obviously twisted may feel his desperate need for God's forgiveness and help; but someone who thinks he's doing everything right feels no need of God or His forgiveness, and so he closes his heart to the very help Jesus came to give.

The poor tax collector prayed, "O God, be merciful to me, for I am a sinner" (Luke 18:13). He saw himself as a wicked man and so did everyone else. But he felt his need, and with his burden of guilt and shame he came before God, pleading for mercy. His heart was open for the

Holy Spirit to do its compassionate work and set him free from his dysfunction. In contrast, the Pharisee's boastful, holier-than-thou prayer showed that his heart was closed to the Spirit's whisper. Because his interests were not in tune with God's, he had no idea his heart was so polluted. He felt no need and he received nothing.

Don't Put It Off!

If you see your sinfulness, don't wait to make yourself better. You may think you aren't good enough yet to come to Jesus. But do you expect to become better through your own efforts? "Can an Ethiopian change the color of his skin? Can a leopard take away his spots? Neither can you start doing good, for you have always done evil" (Jeremiah 13:23). The only way you can change is by God's help. Don't wait to feel more deeply convicted. Don't wait for a better time or to feel more qualified. You can't do it alone. Come to Jesus now, just the way you are.

Don't be deceived by the idea that God is too loving and kind to judge those who reject Him. If that was true, there was no need for Jesus to suffer the horror of the cross. Only look at Jesus on the cross to know that God is serious about eliminating sin. Jesus died for us because there was no other way to save us from the consequences of sin. Without the total surrender of His will and the sacrifice of His own life, it would have been impossible for the human race to escape the deadly power of sin. But He couldn't bear to give us up, and so He took on Himself the guilt of our disobedience and suffered in our place. God in shackles. God impaled on a cross. God dying in agony. The unquenchable love of God for a world twisted and broken by sin! We have no escape from sin's power, no hope of a higher life, except through the surrender of our lives to Jesus who suffered all that to save us.

Those who have not repented sometimes excuse themselves by pointing at so-called Christians and saying, "I'm just as good as they are. They don't act any better than I do. They're into all the same things as I am." They make the faults of others an excuse for their own behavior. But the sins of others don't excuse anyone. God didn't give us a messed up person as a role model. He gave us Jesus, His perfect Son, as our example. Rather than criticizing other people, turn to Jesus and see His perfection. You'll see how much work still needs to be done in you. Then humbly ask Him to heal you.

Don't put it off! Far too many people make that mistake and it costs them everything. Life is short and tomorrow is uncertain. There is a terrible danger—a danger few understand—in waiting to obey God's call. Putting off the decision is actually a decision to remain in sin. And indulging even the smallest sin puts you at risk of losing eternal life forever. What you don't conquer will conquer you.

Adam and Eve convinced themselves that eating the forbidden fruit was no big deal. How could it possibly carry such terrible consequences as God had said? But what seemed trivial to them was actually disobedience of God's eternal and holy law. That first sin separated the human race from God and opened the floodgates of death and grief upon our world. From that day on we have wept in pain, and all creation groans with us as a result of Adam's disobedience. Heaven itself bears the wounds of our rebellion against God. The cross is a memorial of the amazing sacrifice required to pay for our disobedience of the divine law. Let us never think of sin as a trivial, insignificant thing.

Every act of rebellion, every neglect or rejection of the grace of Christ, damages your heart; it makes you unresponsive to Him, it weakens your will, it numbs your conscience, and makes you deaf to the pleading of God's Holy Spirit. Many people think they can change their wrong behavior and bad habits whenever they want. They think they can ignore Jesus' call and expect Him to keep calling. They think that even after despising God's Spirit and joining forces with Satan, if they get desperate, they can still change their direction. But it's not that easy. They are more likely to find that evil has become so much a part of who they are that they never do want to turn it over to Jesus.

Every sin you harbor makes you less interested in God. Unless you surrender all your junk to Him, you will eventually end up rejecting God completely. In all the Bible there is not a more fearful warning against playing around with evil than King Solomon's words: "an evil man is held captive by his own sins; they are ropes that catch and hold him" (Proverbs 5:22).

Jesus is ready to set you free from sin, but He will never force you. If you persistently rebel, if you're determined to do evil, if you don't want to be set free and you won't accept His grace, what more can He do? You will have destroyed yourself by your stubborn rejection of His love. "Indeed, the 'right time' is now. Today is the day of salvation" (2 Corinthians 6:2). "Today when you hear His voice, don't harden your hearts" (Hebrews 3:7,8).

Search Me!

"People judge by outward appearance, but the LORD looks at a person's thoughts and intentions" (1 Samuel 16:7). He sees your conflicting emotions, and He knows you struggle with a heart that is deceitful and twisted. He knows your deepest motives. Go to Him with your life all stained as it is. Throw open your heart to God and say, "Search me, O God, and know my heart; test me and know my thoughts. Point out anything in me that offends You, and lead me along the path of everlasting life" (Psalm 139:23-24). "Create in me a clean heart, O God. Renew a right spirit within me" (Psalm 51:10). Be honest with yourself about the state of your heart. Be as serious as you would be if your physical life were in danger. This is a matter to be settled between God and you for eternity. To just hope you can get by will eventually destroy you.

The Bible will help you in your battle with sin. Study it prayerfully. You will discover that holiness is required. "Those who are not holy will not see the Lord" (Hebrews 12:14). The Bible will convince you of sin, but it will also plainly show you the way God rescues you from sin. Listen and obey what it says as the voice of God speaking to your heart.

Relentless Rescuer

As you see the awfulness of your sin, don't give up in despair. It was sinners that Jesus came to save. You don't have to make peace with God; instead God, through Jesus, is making peace with you. What amazing love! He is "reconciling the world to Himself" (2 Corinthians 5:19). He's romancing the hearts of his rebellious children with His gentle love. No earthly parent could be as patient with the faults and mistakes of his children as God is with those He's trying to save. No one could plead more lovingly with the rebel. No human lips ever poured out sweeter invitations than God does. All His promises and all His warnings are spoken in love.

When Satan tells you that you're too wrong to be made right, too filthy to be made clean, look to Jesus, your rescuer. Talk about Jesus and what He has done for you. It will encourage in the rough times to remember that Jesus has not given up on you, that He loves you, and that He will save you from yourself even now. Admit your mistakes. Admit that you have sinned, but tell the enemy that "Christ Jesus came into the world to save sinners" (1 Timothy 1:15) and that He loves you too much to let anyone tear you away from Him.

Jesus was once a guest in the home of a man named Simon. Simon thought he was better than most people. Jesus told him a story about two men. One owed his master a small amount of money, and the other owed him a very large amount. The master forgave them both. Jesus asked Simon which man would love his master most. Simon answered, "The one for whom he canceled the larger debt" (Luke 7:43). We have been great sinners, but Jesus died so we can be forgiven. His death is more than enough to present to the Father in our behalf. Those He has forgiven most will love Him most. In heaven, you'll want to be as close as possible to the One who has forgiven you so much. You'll adore Him for loving you beyond reason and for sacrificing everything to save you. When you realize that God is crazy about you, you'll know how awful it is to rebel against Him. When you understand something of the enormous sacrifice Jesus made to rescue you, your heart will melt with love and regret. You'll humbly repent and turn your life over to Him.

Discussion Questions

1. Have you felt so ashamed of who you are or what you've done that you don't even dare to hope? What does God say to you?   2 Corinthians 5:19; Acts 26:9-11; 1 Timothy 1:12-16; Isaiah 1:18; John 3:16-18

2. How about the opposite problem? Do you find that you don't usually have a deep sense of shame over the way you think or the things you do? No desperate sense of need to be forgiven and healed? What does God say to you? 1 John 1:10; Revelation 3:15-20; John 16:7, 8; Mark 10:46-52; 1 John 1:7-9

3. Repentance is a gift from God. He gently leads us to it (Acts 5:30, 31; Romans 2:4) by helping us see the full extent of the damage we have caused, because no sin is victimless. At the same time, He helps us see the full extent of the cross, because without the cross, the weight of our shame would destroy us.

   How has God led you to repentance?

4. Have you felt like you couldn't go to God with the stain of guilt all over you? Have you felt that you needed to somehow clean up first? What's wrong with that idea? Jeremiah 13:23

5. Read the story in Luke 7:36-50. Which character do you most relate to? What does Jesus say to you? What is your response?

S T E P 4

We made a searching and fearless moral inventory of our-selves.

"Let us examine our ways and test them, and let us return to the Lord."

~ Lamentations 3:40

Choosing to Admit
What's Wrong
(Confession)

Getting real about the junk in your heart.

P eople who conceal their sins will not prosper, but if they confess and turn from them, they will receive mercy" (Proverbs 28:13).

The conditions of receiving God's forgiveness are simple and fair and reasonable. God doesn't expect you to make a great sacrifice or perform some painful penance in order to prove you're sorry and earn His forgiveness. If you simply confess your sins and choose to leave them behind, God will forgive you fully and freely.

But what are you to confess? And to whom?

Identifying What's Wrong

True confession is always specific—it identifies specific sins. This requires searching your heart and making a fearless inventory of your moral wrongs. As you get real with yourself about the flaws in your make-up which have caused your failures, you'll begin to see exactly what you have done wrong. Some of the sins you will identify are private and you should bring them only before God and, possibly, a compassionate and trustworthy counselor. Some of your sins have caused harm to other people and should be confessed to them. Some sins are public and should be publicly confessed. But all confession should be definite and to the point, acknowledging the exact nature of your wrongs.

The Bible tells how the Hebrew people had rebelled against God and were suffering the results of their sin. They had stopped trusting God to lead and protect them, despite all His care for them in the past. They had rejected the great Ruler of the universe and had insisted on a human king instead so they could be like the nations around them. During their recovery from this rebellion, they made a specific confession: "We have added to our sins by asking for a king" (1 Samuel 12:19). They were convicted by this particular sin and realized their need to confess it. Their ungratefulness had weighed on them and had disconnected them from God.

The apostle James says, "Confess your sins to each other and pray for each other so that you may be healed" (James 5:16). Admit your sins to God. He is the only One who can both forgive you and cleanse your heart. But also confess your faults to each other, and choose to admit what you've done wrong. If you've offended your friend or any other person, tell them you are sorry. For their own recovery, they need the opportunity to forgive you. Then ask God for forgiveness, because you have harmed God's own child. By hurting other people, you sin against God who created them and who is working to rescue them.

When you confess your sins to God, remember that you're coming before Jesus—the only person in the universe who "faced all of the same testings we do, yet He did not sin," and who "understands our weaknesses"(Hebrews 4:15). He not only understands, He is able to remove all the guilt of your sin.

True Confession

Until you've humbled your heart before God and admitted your guilt, you haven't met the first condition of acceptance. If you aren't sorry, if you have no shame or regret, you aren't serious about seeking forgiveness. And if you've never really wanted to be forgiven, it's certain you haven't found peace with God. Confession isn't about saying the words. It's about humbly admitting to God that you were wrong and that you deeply desire to be right with Him. That is the only condition you must meet. And that's why no one should twist your arm and force you to confess. Make your confession only after you have recognized your sin and truly repented. Then you can be sure that God, who loves you with such deep compassion, will accept your confession with open arms. David, the psalm writer, says, "The Lord is close to the brokenhearted; he rescues those who are crushed in spirit" (Psalm 34:18).

When you're really sorry for your sin, you'll make definite changes in your life; you'll cut out the wrong habits and all the things that tempt you to go back. God says: "Give up your evil ways. Learn to do good." (Isaiah 1:16). If the wicked "return what they have stolen, and obey my life-giving laws, no longer doing what is evil. If they do this, then they will surely live and not die" (Ezekiel 33:15). The apostle Paul encouraged his friends in their repentance: "Just see what this godly sorrow produced in you! Such earnestness, such concern to clear yourselves, such indignation, such alarm, such longing to see me, such zeal, and such a readiness to punish wrong. You showed that you have done everything necessary to make things right" (2 Corinthians 7:11).

Excuses and Blame

As long as sin numbs your awareness of right and wrong, you won't see how your character is twisted. You won't realize the extent of the damage you've done. Until you surrender to the convicting power of the Holy Spirit, you'll remain partially blind to your sin. Your confessions won't be sincere. Even if you do admit your guilt, you may find yourself adding an excuse: "If it hadn't been for this or that, I wouldn't have done it."

Adam and Eve were like that. After they ate the forbidden fruit, they felt ashamed and afraid. They made excuses hoping to avoid their fate. Adam blamed his wife for tempting him, and he blamed God for giving him such a wife. "It was the woman you gave me who brought me the fruit, and I ate it." Eve blamed the snake, "'the serpent tricked me,' she replied, 'that's why I ate it.'" (Genesis 3:12,13). Why did You make the serpent? Why did You let him to come into Eden? Their questions show that Adam and Eve were actually trying to shift the blame of their rebellion to God in order to excuse themselves. They learned that trick from Satan, the one who had deceived them.

Coming Clean

Satan, the inventor of lies, was the first to justify himself by blaming someone else for his wrong. People have been doing the same thing ever since our first parents listened to him. That's not the kind of confession the Holy Spirit will lead you to make. He'll lead you to accept your own guilt and admit it without any lies or cover-ups. You'll be like the man praying in the temple who was too ashamed to even look up to heaven and cried out, "God, be merciful to me a sinner!" (Luke 18:13). And when you admit your guilt, God will immediately forgive you. Jesus will present His sacrifice on your behalf and will take your guilt on Himself.

The examples in God's Word of true repentance and humility show a spirit of confession in which there is no excuse for sin and no attempt at self-defense. Look how Paul describes his sin in its worst light, with no excuse or blame: "Authorized by the leading priests, I caused many believers there to be sent to prison. And I cast my vote against them when they were condemned to death. Many times I had them punished in the synagogues to get them to curse Jesus. I was so violently opposed to them that I even chased them down in foreign cities" (Acts 26:10-11). He doesn't hesitate to announce to everyone that "Christ Jesus came into the world to save sinners—and I am the worst of them all" (1 Timothy 1:15).

When you sincerely repent, your heart will be humble and broken and you'll have some sense of the immense love of God and the infinite cost of the cross. Then nothing will be able to stop you from coming clean to God—the Father who loves you. And the Bible says, "If we confess our sins to Him, He is faithful and just to forgive us our sins and to cleanse us from all wickedness" (1 John 1:9).

That's a promise you can count on!

Discussion Questions

1. As a child, were you ever forced to say sorry? What is wrong with being forced to do that?

2. In this chapter you read:

    As long as sin numbs your awareness of right and wrong, you won't see how your character is twisted. You won't realize the extent of the damage you've done. Until you surrender to the convicting power of the Holy Spirit, you'll remain partially blind to your sin. Your confessions won't be sincere. Even if you do admit your guilt, you may find yourself adding an excuse: "If it hadn't been for this or that, I wouldn't have done it."

    Are you convicted of your sin and your need to be forgiven? What brought you to this point?

3. Paul, a man of God, described what some of his friends did after they had repented (2 Corinthians 7:11). From their example, what do you see that you need to do in your journey of repentance and confession?

4. What does confession look like when it's real? What does the writer mean about being washed clean? Which part of his confession means the most to you? Why? Psalm 32:1-5; Psalm 51:1-17

5. Besides confessing to God, who else may you need to confess to? James 5:16.

    Why is this necessary? Exodus 19:5

6. What two things does God promise to do when you confess? Why are both so important? 1 John 1:9

7. Write your own prayer of confession, using some of the prayers from question 4 as a model.

S T 5 E P

We admitted to God, to ourselves, and to another human being the exact nature of our wrongs.

"Therefore, confess your sins to one another and pray for each other that you may be healed."
                                                      ~ *James 5:16*

CHAPTER 5

Sold Out to Jesus

(Consecration)

Surrender to God is the pathway to sanity.

God has promised, "If you look for me wholeheartedly, you will find me" (Jeremiah 29:13).

With God, it's all or nothing. Surrendering your heart to God is like breathing—either you do or you don't. Until you turn your life over to God to be restored, your heart won't change. By nature, all of us are alienated against God. The Holy Spirit says you are "dead because of your disobedience and your many sins" (Ephesians 2:1); "your head is injured, and your heart is sick. You are sick from head to foot" (Isaiah 1:5, 6); You're caught in Satan's trap, "held captive by him to do whatever he wants" (2 Timothy 2:26). The good news is that God yearns to heal you and set you free. But since this requires a complete change—a renewing of everything you are—it only happens when you completely surrender to Him.

The struggle to turn it all over to God is the greatest battle you'll ever fight. Giving up your rights, surrendering everything to God's will, isn't easy; but when you turn your will over to Him and repent of your sin and admit what's wrong, He will heal you and restore you to sanity.

It's Your Choice

Satan wants you to think that God forces people to follow Him without thinking for themselves. But God is not like that at all. He created you with a mind to think and with the ability and freedom to choose. He says, "Come now, let's settle this," let's "reason together" (Isaiah 1:18). God doesn't force you to do anything. He doesn't want you to worship Him or obey Him unless you choose to do so. If God forced you to surrender to Him, you'd be a robot. That has never been His plan. Humans are the crowning work of God's creation. He wants you to fulfill the highest potential He placed within you. He longs to give you a beautiful life filled with His greatest blessings. God invites you to give yourself to Him so He can work His good will in you. It is left for you to choose whether you'll stay in the prison of sin or share in the wonderful freedom God provides for His children.

Giving your heart to God means giving up everything that separates you from Him. Jesus says, "You cannot become my disciple without giving up everything you own" (Luke 14:33). He doesn't mean that He won't let you follow Him, but that you won't be able to follow Him until you give up everything that turns your heart away from Him. The desire for wealth handcuffs many people to Satan. Some are obsessed with power and success while others want the easy life with no responsibility. A life of immorality and addiction captures others. But these chains must be broken. You can't be half the Lord's and half the world's. You aren't God's child at all unless you're His completely.

There are people who say they serve God, but actually are depending on their own efforts to become good and earn a ticket to heaven. They don't admit that they're powerless to change. Their hearts aren't convicted by any deep awareness of Jesus' love or His desire to restore them. They haven't turned their lives over to Him or admitted their wrongs or their need of a Savior. Instead, they try to be perfect, thinking this will get them to heaven. But this sort of religion is worth nothing.

When you turn your life over to Jesus, you'll be so filled with His love and the joy of being with Him that you'll never want to let go of Him. Jesus will become your highest priority. Everything you do, you'll do for Him. When His love fills your heart, you won't ask how little you can do. You won't try to get by with the lowest standard, but will do your absolute best to please Him. You'll gladly give up anything because He means everything to you. On the other hand, trying to "do right" without Jesus' love in your heart will leave you thirsty, empty, and exhausted.

An Amazing Deal

Do you feel it's too big a sacrifice to give everything over to Jesus? Ask yourself, "What has Jesus given for me?" The Son of God gave His very life to save you. Every second of your life you are blessed by the kindness of God. It's because He protects you from so many of Satan's attacks that you don't fully realize the depths of misery you would experience without Him. Saving you from the results of your sin cost Him everything. Can you think about what He went through to save you and just shrug it off? Can you think of all He does for you and still hold yourself back from Him?

Many people ask, "Why do I have to humble myself and be sorry before I can be sure God accepts me?" Just look at Jesus. He was sinless, and more than that, He was the Prince of heaven. But to rescue us, He actually took on all the guilt of sin for the human race. "He was counted among the rebels. He bore the sins of many and interceded for rebels" (Isaiah 53:12). But what do we give up, when we surrender everything? We give up a heart polluted by sin, and Jesus gives us back a life purified through His death and saved by His incomparable love. What an unbelievable deal! How can anyone think it's hard to surrender to Him?

God doesn't demand that you give up anything good. He never wants anything but the best for you. What He offers is much better than what you seek for yourself. Rebelling against Him will only hurt you. You can never be happy running away from Him. He knows the way to happiness and peace. The path of rebellion and selfishness is the path to misery and destruction.

Don't think for a minute that God wants to see you suffer. Everyone is heaven is interested in your happiness. Your heavenly Father never deprives you of anything that will bring you joy. He urges you to have nothing to do with the things that separate you from Him because they will only hurt you. Jesus welcomes you just the way you are, with all your needs, faults, and weaknesses, but He doesn't leave you that way. When you surrender to Him, He removes your guilt and rescues you from Satan's prison. He satisfies the longings of your heart and gives you peace and rest. Jesus only asks you to do those things that will bring you the greatest joy—a joy known only by those who surrender to Him.

The Power of the Will

Are you wondering, "How do I surrender to God?" You want to give yourself to Him, but you feel weak and troubled by doubt. Your bad habits control you. Your promises and good intentions are like ropes of sand. You can't control your thoughts, your desires, or your feelings. The knowledge of your broken promises makes you doubt your own sincerity and feel that God can't accept you.

Don't give up! What you need is to understand the true force of the will—your power of choice. It controls every aspect of your life. Everything depends on your choices. God gave you the power of choice. You can use it to help you or to harm you. While you can't change your heart on your own or remove your rebellious tendencies, you can choose to serve God. You can give Him your will. Then your whole nature will be brought under the control of His Spirit. God can change your heart so that His goals become your goals and His desires become your desires.

Wanting to be right with God is fine; but if you stop there, it won't do you any good. Many people will be lost while hoping and desiring to be right. They don't come to the point of giving up their will to God. They don't choose to surrender to Him. But if you do choose Him, you'll see a total change in your life. By turning over your will to Jesus, you join yourself with the greatest power in the universe. You'll have strength from God to help you stand firm. Through constant surrender to God you'll live a new life—a life of trusting Him.

Discussion Questions

1. You'll find that you have to repent and confess over and over as you reconnect to God. That's because, like every other person, you're naturally rebellious against God. How does the Bible describe our condition? Ephesians 2:1; Isaiah 1:5, 6, 2 Timothy 2:26

   What do you see in yourself that fits this description?

2. God didn't create us as wounded slaves of Satan or our addictions. He created us as His children with characters like His. He wants to rescue us, heal us, and help us to laugh out loud in our own skin. What must you do so He can do that for you? James 4:7-10; Hebrews 12:4-13

   Are you ready to do that?

3. What did Jesus say it is not possible to do? Luke 14:33; Luke 16:13

   Have you experienced the truth of what He said? Share about that.

4. How does God describe the things He asks you to give up? What does He offer you instead?   Isaiah 55:1-3, 6-7

   What do you most long for? What are some of the ways that you have tried to satisfy the thirst of your soul? What has been the result?

5. What do you see in your life that prevents you from giving yourself to Jesus?

6. How can you surrender totally to God? Deuteronomy 30:19, 20; Psalm 139:23, 24; Philippians 2:13

7. Have you tried giving God your will? How did you see Him work in your life? Share an example.

STEP 6

We were entirely ready to have God remove all these defects of character.

"Humble yourselves before the Lord and He will lift you up."

~ James 4:10

A Place to Belong
(Faith and Acceptance)

Accepting God's forgiveness and healing of your shortcomings.

As the Holy Spirit wakes up your conscience, sin will appear more evil to you. You'll see its power and you'll hate the guilt and heartache it causes. You'll see that sin has separated you from God and you'll realize that you're a slave to the power of evil. The more you struggle to escape, the more you realize your helplessness. Your motives aren't good; your heart is not clean. You see that your life has been filled with selfishness and sin. You are entirely ready to give up all the defects in your character. You long to be forgiven, to be clean, to be set free. You want to live in harmony with God and be like Him, but how can you ever do that?

I'm Willing—Now What?

Peace is what you need. Heaven's forgiveness, peace, and love in your heart. You can't buy it with money or

67

earn it with your best effort; you can't be smart enough or "enlightened" enough to reach it. You can never hope, by your own efforts, to have peace in your soul. Instead, God offers it to you as a gift. "It's all free!" (Isaiah 55:1). It's yours if you just hold out your hands to receive it. God says, "Though your sins are like scarlet, I will make them as white as snow. Though they are red like crimson, I will make them as white as wool" (Isaiah 1:18). "And I will give you a new heart, and I will put a new spirit in you. I will take out your stony, stubborn heart and give you a tender, responsive heart" (Ezekiel 36:26).

You're now at the point where you've confessed your sins and in your heart you want them out of your life for good. You have committed to give yourself to God. So next, talk to Him—pray to Him. Ask Him to remove your sins and heal you of your addictions. Ask Him to give you a new desire to live life for Him. Then believe that He does this because He has promised it. Jesus taught this lesson while He was on earth. He promises us that when we believe, God will heal us.

He is Able to Heal You

Jesus healed people of their diseases when they had faith in His power. He helped them to believe because they could see Him healing people right in front of their eyes. When they saw that He could heal them physically, they also began to trust Him to heal them spiritually. Because He healed them on the outside, Jesus showed them He could heal them on the inside as well. He has the power to forgive sins. He clearly explained this when He healed the man sick with paralysis: "'So I will prove to you that the Son of Man has the authority on earth to forgive sins.' Then Jesus turned to the paralyzed man and said, 'Stand up, pick up your mat, and go home!'" (Matthew 9:6). Jesus' disciple, John, wrote about the miracles of Jesus "so that you may continue to believe that Jesus is the Messiah, the Son of God, and that by believing in him you will have life by the power of his name" (John 20:31).

From the examples in the Bible of how Jesus healed the sick, you can learn to trust that He is able to forgive your sins. Another Bible story about a man Jesus healed helps us to understand the connection between our belief and His power. This man was paralyzed. He had not used his arms or legs for thirty-eight years. When Jesus saw the man, He told him, "Stand up, pick up your mat, and walk!" (John 5:8). The sick man might have said, "Lord, if You will make me well, I will obey You." But no; he believed Jesus' words, he believed he was healed, and he made the effort to get up right away. He decided to walk, and he did. He acted on the command of Jesus, and God gave the power to heal him.

In a similar way, you are also paralyzed from your sins. You can't correct your past life; you can't change your heart or heal your soul. But God promises to do all this for you through Jesus. You can believe that promise. You can confess your sins and turn your life over to God. You can decide to serve Him. As soon as you do this, God will make His promise to you a reality. If you believe the promise—believe that you're forgiven and made clean—God will make it true. You're healed spiritually when you believe, just as Jesus gave the paralyzed man the power to walk when the man believed he was healed. It is true, if you believe it.

Don't wait to feel you're forgiven. Just say, "I believe it; it is true, not because I feel it, but because God has promised it."

Jesus says, "You can pray for anything, and if you believe that you've received it, it will be yours" (Mark 11:24). There is a condition to this promise—that you pray according to God's will. But it is God's will to forgive you, to heal you from sin, and to restore your sanity. So you can ask for these things, believe that you receive them, and thank God that you have received them. It's your privilege to go to Jesus and be forgiven, to stand before God's law without shame, guilt free. "So now there is no condemnation for those who belong to Christ Jesus. And because you belong to him, the power of the life-giving Spirit has freed you from the power of sin that leads to death" (Romans 8:1).

From now on, you are not your own. You were bought with a price. "For you know that God paid a ransom to save you from the empty life you inherited from your ancestors, and the ransom he paid was not mere gold or silver. It was the precious blood of Christ, the sinless, spotless Lamb of God" (1 Peter 1:18-19). Through this simple act of believing God, a new life has been born in your heart through the Holy Spirit. You're a child born into God's family, and He loves you as much as He loves His Son.

Staying on Track

Now that you've turned your life over to Jesus, don't fall back, don't turn away from Him. Every day say, "I belong to Jesus. I have given myself to Him." Ask Him to give you His Spirit, and to keep you on track and keep you from sinning. It was when you turned your life over to God that you became His, and it's by continuing to turn it over to Him that you remain His. The apostle Paul says, "And now, just as you accepted Christ Jesus as your Lord, you must continue to follow him" (Colossians 2:6).

Some people feel that they must be on probation and must prove to God that they have changed their lives before they can receive God's help. But the truth is that you can claim God's blessing and help right now. You need the power of the Holy Spirit to help with your weaknesses or you can't resist evil at all. Jesus loves to have you come to Him just as you are: sinful, helpless, and dependent. He wants you to come to Him with all the stuff you've done wrong, to bring your twisted junk and fall at His feet in true regret for what you've done. He wants to wrap you in His arms, bandage the wounds caused by your sin, and cleanse you from your addictions and impurity.

Many people get hung up right here—they don't believe Jesus forgives them. They don't take God at His word and trust Him. But the truth is that when you repent, confess, and surrender to God, you can know for sure that God freely forgives every sin. Don't believe God's promises are not meant for you. They are for every person who is sorry for their sins. Jesus sends angels to give you strength to help you in your battle with sin. You can never sin so much that you can't find help in Jesus. He died for you! He wants more than anything to clean up your ruined life and throw out your sins, like stained and filthy clothes. He will cover you with His perfect life, like a white robe of righteousness. He invites you to live and not die.

The Incredible Compassion of God

God doesn't treat you the same way people do. He thinks of you constantly and all His thoughts are filled with a yearning compassion. He says, "Let the wicked change their ways and banish the very thought of doing wrong. Let them turn to the LORD that he may have mercy on them. Yes, turn to our God, for he will forgive generously" (Isaiah 55:7); "I have swept away your sins like a cloud. I have scattered your offenses like the morning mist. Oh, return to me, for I have paid the price to set you free" (Isaiah 44:22). "I don't want you to die, says the Sovereign LORD. Turn back and live!" (Ezekiel 18:32).

Satan is ready to steal your trust in God's promises. He wants to rob you of all hope. Don't let him! Don't listen to his lies. Say, "Jesus died so I can live. He loves me, and He doesn't want me to die. I have a compassionate Father in heaven."

Jesus told a story about a young man who ran away from home. He ended up in a really bad place and lost everything he had. He recognized his mistakes and longed to return home to his father. You can do the same thing that young man did. You can say, "Although I have abused God's love, although I have wasted the good things He's given me, I will get up and go back to my Father." Like him you can say, "'I have sinned against both heaven and You, and I am no longer worthy of being called your [child]. Please take me on as a hired servant.'" Jesus told this story to show you how God will receive you when you turn back to Him: "While he was still a long way off, his father saw him coming. Filled with love and compassion, he ran to his son, embraced him, and kissed him" (Luke 15:18-20).

But even this story, tender and touching as it is, comes short of getting across the incredible compassion of your heavenly Father. God says, "I have loved you, my people, with an everlasting love. With unfailing love I have drawn you to myself" (Jeremiah 31:3). While the sinner is still miles away from his Father's house, wasting all his money in a foreign country, the Father's heart is aching over him. Every longing in your heart to return to God is actually the voice of God's Spirit, tenderly pleading with you. Like a gentle, caring Father, He is trying to inviting you, drawing you to return to Hi

With the rich promises of the Bible before you, doubt? Can you really believe the Lord would be harsh and stop His child from coming to Him in repentance when you long to forsake your sins and return? He says, "Never! Can a mother forget her nursing child? Can she feel no love for the child she has borne? But even if that were possible, I would not forget you!" (Isaiah 49:15). Nothing can cause more damage to your soul than to believe such a lie about your heavenly Father. He hates sin, but He loves the sinner. He gave Himself, in the person of Jesus, so that anyone who wants to be saved can have peace and joy with Him forever.

Look up to Heaven when you doubt and are afraid, because Jesus lives to step in and intervene for you. Thank God for the gift of His precious Son and pray that His death for you was not wasted. The Spirit invites you today. Come with your whole heart to Jesus and claim His blessing.

As you read God's promises, remember He gave them to assure you that He is crazy about you. He is drawn to sinners with a compassion that knows no boundaries. "He is so rich in kindness and grace that he purchased our freedom with the blood of his Son and forgave our sins" (Ephesians 1:7). Believe that God is your helper. He wants to restore His moral image in you. As you draw near to Him with confession and repentance, He will draw near to you with mercy and forgiveness.

Discussion Questions

1. Share how you have struggled with the idea that God cannot forgive you. What finally brought you to the point of being able to accept that He does?

2. Does Jesus have the power to forgive you for the damage you've done? How do you know? Matthew 9:1-8

3. How can you be sure God forgives you? 1 John 5:14, 15; John 6:40; Ezekiel 33:10, 11

4. How thoroughly does God respond when you ask forgiveness? 1 John 1:9; Isaiah 1:18; Isaiah 55:7; Isaiah 44:22; Romans 8:1, Zephaniah 3:17

5. Have you despaired of ever overcoming the junk inside your heart? Share a little of that experience.

   What encouragement do you find in these verses? Luke 15:11-24; Romans 5:10; 2 Corinthians 5:18-20; Ephesians 2:3-5, 13

6. How are you responding right now to God, knowing He loves you so much, and is so eager desire to rescue you, forgive you, and heal you?

S T **7** E P

We humbly asked Him to remove all our shortcomings.

"If we confess our sins He is faithful and just and will forgive us our sins and purify us from all unrighteousness."

~ 1 John 1:9

7

Following Jesus
(The Test of Discipleship)

Stick close to Jesus as He removes the defects in your character.

Anyone who belongs to Christ has become a new person. The old life is gone; a new life has begun!" (2 Corinthians 5:17).

You may not be able to pinpoint the exact time or place, or tell precisely the chain of events in the process of your conversion, but this doesn't mean that you have not turned to God. Jesus said, "The wind blows wherever it wants. Just as you can hear the wind but can't tell where it comes from or where it is going, so you can't explain how people are born of the Spirit" (John 3:8). Although you can't see it, you can feel the wind blow and see what it does. That's how it is when God's Spirit works in your heart. You can't see Him do it, but He sparks a new life in your soul; He removes the defects in your character and creates a new inner self modeled after God's character. Even though the Spirit works behind the scenes, everyone can see the result of His work.

A Change of Character

If your heart has been renewed by the Holy Spirit, your life will show it. You can't remove the defects in your own character or bring yourself into harmony with God, but your life will show whether you have surrendered yourself to God's Spirit. People will see a change in your character, your habits, and your interests. The difference between what you used to be and what you are now will be obvious. People will know your character, not by occasional good or bad behavior, but by how you speak and act every day.

Be careful, though, about putting on an act without actually surrendering to Jesus and letting Him change you. To protect your reputation or to earn respect you might live what looks like a decent life. Self-respect might motivate you to avoid anything that looks bad. You might act generously even though you're actually selfish. So how can you know whose side you're really on? The key is to notice what's going on inside your head. Who has your heart? Who do you think about? Who do you love to talk about? Who do you love most and who are you most willing to follow? If you belong to Jesus, He'll be your first priority and your sweetest thoughts will be of Him. You'll dedicate all you have and everything you are to Him. You'll long to act like Him, obey Him, and please Him in everything.

When the Holy Spirit makes you a new person in Christ Jesus you'll grow more and more like Him. When you stay connected to Jesus, you'll be filled with "love, joy, peace, patience, kindness, goodness, faithfulness, gentleness, and self-control" (Galatians 5:22,23). You won't live like you used to, indulging your addictions and dysfunctions. Instead, if you trust Jesus, you'll follow in His steps, reflect His character, and turn away from sources that lead you to addictive behaviors. The things you once hated, you will now love, and the things you once loved, you will now hate. Instead of being proud and arrogant, you'll become humble. Instead of giving in to your addiction, you'll become clean and sober. Instead of immoral behavior, you'll become moral. You won't go along with the crowd just to fit in. You won't "be concerned about the outward beauty," but you'll be very eager to have "the beauty that comes from within, the unfading beauty of a gentle and quiet spirit" (1 Peter 3:3,4).

The evidence of genuine repentance is change. You can tell the Spirit has been at work in you when you start keeping your promises, paying back what you've stolen, confessing your sins, and loving God and everyone else. When you come to Jesus as a guilty, sinful person, and receive His forgiveness and undeserved kindness, you'll love Him deeply. Every trouble will seem easier to deal with when Jesus is with you. Doing your duty will become your delight. You'll be glad to sacrifice your time, money, and energy for Him. Your path that once was so dark will be bright with the light of Jesus' presence.

As you humbly ask God to remove your shortcomings, the Spirit will create Christ's lovely character traits in you. Jesus loved to obey God. The most important thing in His life was to bring honor to God. Love made all His actions beautiful. Love is from God. A heart that is not dedicated to God can't love well. Only as you humbly receive God's love will you truly love other people. "We love each other because He loved us first" (1 John 4:19). As the Spirit changes you, love will influence everything you do. Love will soften your character, control your desires and passions, free you from anger and bitterness, and make you kind and unselfish. The more you love others, the sweeter your life will be, and the more you'll influence those around you for the better.

The Two Mistakes

There are two mistakes you especially need to avoid — particularly when you're new to trusting Jesus. The first is trying to be good enough to earn God's favor. Remember that it's impossible to become good enough by your own efforts. Without Jesus, everything you do is polluted with selfishness and sin. It is only by trusting in Jesus and His sacrifice that you can be made holy.

The second mistake is the opposite of the first, and just as dangerous. This mistake is thinking that if you believe in Jesus you don't have to keep God's law (the Ten Commandments). Many people believe their behavior has nothing to do with being saved since it truly is by faith alone that we share in the grace of Christ. But notice here that obedience is not just about your outward actions. Real obedience comes from the heart. Real obedience is the way you act because you love Jesus.

The law of God is a description of how a person will behave when their character is like God's. It shows what it looks like to be a loving person. God's government of the whole universe is based on that kind of love. If God is removing the defects in your character and changing you to be like Jesus, won't you want to obey His law of love? As God's love grows in your heart, His promise is fulfilled: "I will put My laws in their hearts so they will understand them, and I will write them on their minds so they will obey them" (Hebrews 10:16). And if God's law is written on your heart, won't it show in your actions? The surest sign that you love Jesus is that you obey Him.

The Bible says, "Loving God means keeping His commandments" (1 John 5:3); and "If someone claims, 'I know God,' but doesn't obey God's commandments, that person is a liar and is not living in the truth" (1 John 2:4). Instead of excusing you from obedience, faith enables you to obey.

The True Test

You don't earn salvation by obeying. Salvation is the free gift of God and you receive it by faith. But obedience is the result of faith. "You know that Jesus came to take away our sins, and there is no sin in him. Anyone who continues to live in him will not sin. But anyone who keeps on sinning does not know him or understand who he is" (1 John 3:5-6). This is the true test. If you stay close to Jesus and are filled with His love, you'll live your life to please Him. Your feelings, your thoughts, your plans and your actions will be right in line with His will for you. "Dear children, don't let anyone deceive you about this: When people do what is right, it shows that they are righteous, even as Christ is righteous" (1 John 3:7). The Ten Commandments illustrate what it looks like to obey God's holy law—they illustrate what it looks like to love God and each other.

That so-called faith which claims to free people from the need to obey God, is not faith, but presumption. "God saved you by his grace when you believed" (Ephesians 2:8). But "faith by itself isn't enough. Unless it produces good deeds, it is dead and useless" (James 2:17). Before He came to earth, Jesus said this about Himself: "I take joy in doing your will, my God, for your law is written on my heart" (Psalm 40:8). And just before He returned to heaven He told His followers, "When you obey my commandments, you remain in my love, just as I obey my Father's commandments and remain in his love" (John 15:10). The Bible says, "We can be sure that we know him if we obey his commandments. If someone claims, 'I know

God,' but doesn't obey God's commandments, that person is a liar and is not living in the truth. But those who obey God's word truly show how completely they love him. That is how we know we are living in him. Those who say they live in God should live their lives as Jesus did" (1 John 2:3-6). "For God called you to do good, even if it means suffering, just as Christ suffered for you. He is your example, and you must follow in his steps" (1 Peter 2:21).

The requirement for eternal life is the same as it's always been—the same as it was in the garden of Eden before Adam and Eve sinned: Perfect obedience to the law of God. If God gave eternal life to anyone who didn't meet this condition, the happiness of the whole universe would be in danger. Sin, with all its sorrow and misery, would last forever.

Help for the Helpless

It was possible for Adam, before he disobeyed, to have a perfect character and perfectly obey God's law. But he rebelled, and his character became warped. We inherited the same twisted character and our natural tendencies are also to disobey God. We can't make ourselves good. Because we're sinful and unholy, we can't perfectly obey the holy law, the Ten Commandments. We have no goodness or strength of our own to fully obey God's law. But Jesus has made a way of escape for us. He lived on earth and experienced all the same trouble and temptations that we do. But He lived a sinless life. He died for us, and now He offers to take our sins and give us His goodness. If you give yourself to Him and accept Him as your Savior, then, sinful as your life has been, for His sake you're considered holy and guilt-free. Christ's character takes the place of your character, and you're accepted before God just as if you had not sinned.

More than this, Jesus changes your heart. As you surrender to Him, your heart beats in sync with His. You can keep this connection with Jesus by trusting Him constantly and by continually turning over your feelings, desires, and plans to Him. As long as you do this, He will continue changing you, so that soon you will actually want to obey Him. Then you can say, "It is no longer I who live, but Christ lives in me" (Galatians 2:20). Jesus said to His disciples, "It is not you who will be speaking—it will be the Spirit of your Father speaking through you" (Matthew 10:20). With Jesus working in you, you'll have the same attitude as His and you'll do the same things—good and right things.

When you realize your great need of Jesus, you won't feel superior to others. You'll see that all your hope depends on the goodness of Jesus, credited to you, and the work of His Spirit to change your heart.

Trust Your Teacher

Here's an important concept to understand about faith: There is a kind of belief which is completely different than faith. Even Satan and his evil angels acknowledge the existence and power of God and the truth of His Word. The Bible says "Even the demons believe and tremble in terror," but this is not faith (James 2:19).

You have true faith when you believe in God's Word and turn your life over to Him. When you surrender your emotions and desires to God, that's faith—a faith that works by love and makes your soul pure. That kind of faith humbly asks God to change your heart to be like His. Your heart previously didn't know God and couldn't obey His law, but now you delight in His holy commands.

When your heart is changed, you'll say, "Oh, how I love your instructions! I think about them all day long" (Psalm 119:97). Others will see proof that God's ways are good when they see the lives of "those who belong to Christ Jesus. And because you belong to Him, the power of the life-giving Spirit has freed you from the power of sin that leads to death" (Romans 8:1, 2).

Your Rescuer

Some people have experienced God's forgiveness and love, and want with all their hearts to be God's children. But when they look at how they've messed up, and when they see all their faults, they doubt the Holy Spirit has really changed their hearts. If you feel this way, don't despair. Don't give up hope! We all have times when we need to bow down in prayer and cry out to Jesus because of our weaknesses and mistakes, but God does not want us to be discouraged. Even if you give in to Satan's temptations, God won't reject you; He won't abandon you. Far from it! Jesus is "sitting in the place of honor at God's right hand, pleading for us" (Romans 8:34).

Jesus' disciple John said, "I am writing this to you so that you will not sin. But if anyone does sin, we have an advocate who pleads our case before the Father. He is Jesus Christ, the one who is truly righteous" (1 John 2:1). Jesus encourages us, "The Father Himself loves you dearly" (John 16:27). God wants to bring you back to Himself; He wants to see His own purity and holiness reflected in you. If you choose to surrender yourself to Him, He "who began the good work within you, will continue his work until it is finally finished on the day when Christ Jesus returns" (Philippians 1:6). Keep praying and trusting Him. When you finally realize you can't do it on your own, you'll start to trust the power of your Rescuer instead.

The closer you come to Jesus, the more you'll see your own faults. Your vision will be clearer, and your flaws will be seen in stark contrast to His perfection. When this happens, take courage that Satan's lies are losing their power and that the Holy Spirit is working in your life. Deep love for Jesus can only exist in a heart that realizes its own sinfulness. When Jesus changes you, you'll admire His perfect character. But if you're blind to your own failures and the sin in your heart, it is clear evidence that you have not really seen the true beauty and excellence of Jesus.

The less you see to admire in yourself, the more you'll admire the purity and loveliness of Jesus. Seeing your sinfulness leads you into the arms of the One who forgives you. When you see your helplessness and reach out to Jesus, He will show Himself to be your powerful helper. The more your need drives you to Him, the more you'll understand how wonderful He is, and the more you'll become like Him.

Discussion Questions

1. How does Jesus say you can recognize His followers? John 15:14-17

   How well does that description fit you right now?

2. Since you became a follower of Jesus, what change has occurred in your thoughts, interests, choices, and the way you spend your time and money?

3. What analogy did Jesus use to describe His followers? Matthew 5:14-16

4. Even after he gave himself to God, Paul wrote of his ongoing struggle with the sinful desires in his head.

   Can you relate? Share a specific example.

5. What do Paul and other Bible writers tell us about how to handle this struggle? Romans 7:24, 25; Psalm 143:10; Romans 8:5, 6, 13, 14, 26

S T E P

We made a list of all persons we had harmed and became willing to make amends to them all.

"Do unto others as you would have them do to you."

~ Luke 6:31

CHAPTER

Second Childhood
(Growing Up Into Christ)

The Holy Spirit leads you to make amends and begin a new life.

Your recovery and spiritual healing require a change of heart. The Holy Spirit removes the defects in your character and replaces them with the character traits of Jesus. This process is like a birth, or like a farmer's seed, sprouting and growing in the ground. Those who have recently chosen to follow Jesus are "like newborn babies" (1 Peter 2:2), "growing in every way more and more like Christ" (Ephesians 4:15). Like a seed planted in a garden, you'll grow and your character will become more and more like Jesus' character. Those who grow spiritually mature are "like great oaks that the LORD has planted for his own glory" (Isaiah 61:3). In nature you can see many examples to help you understand how spiritual growth works.

What Causes You to Grow?

No human wisdom or skill can create even the simplest form of life. It's only through the power of God that plants and animals live. And it's only by God's power that spiritual life is born in human hearts. "Unless you are born again, you cannot see the Kingdom of God" (John 3:3). Without this new birth, you can't have the eternal life Jesus came to give. God's Spirit has been working in you to give you that new birth. He led you to admit that your life is unmanageable. He helped you to believe that God can restore you to sanity. He encouraged you to turn your life over to Him. Now you have begun a new life with Him.

Growth happens in the same way that life began. God is the One who makes the buds open and the flowers produce fruit. It's by His power the seed develops, "first a leaf blade pushes through, then the heads of wheat are formed, and finally the grain ripens" (Mark 4: 28). The prophet Hosea says of God's people that they "will blossom like the lily...They will flourish like grain and blossom like grapevines" (Hosea 14:5,7). Jesus tells us to "Look at the lilies and how they grow" (Luke 12:27). The plants and flowers don't grow by their own effort, but by receiving what God gives to support life. Children can't make themselves grow taller by straining or worrying. By your own worry or effort, you can't grow spiritually either. It's because of the Holy Spirit that you have come to see your wrongs, to admit them, and to ask God to forgive you and remove the flaws in your character. And it's under the influence of the Holy Spirit that you can now become willing to make amends to those you have harmed. Each step of your spiritual growth and healing happens because you respond to the influence of the Spirit on your heart.

Both plants and children grow by receiving air, sunshine, and food. In the same way, Jesus gives life to you when you trust in Him. He is your "everlasting light" (Isaiah 60:19), a "sun and shield" (Psalm 84:11). He's like "a refreshing dew from heaven" (Hosea 14:5). He refreshes you "like spring rain on freshly cut grass" (Psalm 72:6). He's the living water that satisfies your thirst, "the true Bread of God...who comes down from heaven and gives life to the world" (John 6:33). His gentle kindness is the life of your soul. Breathe in His love so you can live and grow! Just as flowers turn to the bright light of the sun, you can turn to Jesus to grow beautiful and strong like Him. When Jesus' light shines on you, your character will become like His.

Jesus says, "Remain in me, and I will remain in you. For a branch cannot produce fruit if it is severed from the vine, and you cannot be fruitful unless you remain in me... For apart from me you can do nothing" (John 15:4,5). You need Jesus in order to live a holy life, just like a branch needs the main stem, or vine, to grow and produce fruit. Separated from Jesus you have no life. You have no power to resist temptation or to grow in grace and holiness. Living connected to Him, you will thrive. Drawing your energy from Him, you won't shrivel up or be unproductive. You'll be like a tree "planted along the riverbank" (Psalm 1:3), constantly refreshed by the cool water.

What Should You Do?

Many people think they have to do some part of the work of spiritual growth on their own. They trusted Jesus to forgive their sin, but now they try to live good lives by their own efforts. That approach never works. Jesus says, "Apart from me you can do nothing." The only way to grow or be happy or help anyone else is by staying with Jesus. Talk with Him every day, every hour. It's when you're constantly with Him that you grow. He is the one "who initiates and perfects our faith" (Hebrews 12:2). It's

Jesus first and last and always. You need Him with you, not only at the beginning and the end of your life, but every step of the way. The Bible says, "I know the LORD is always with me. I will not be shaken, for he is right beside me" (Psalm 16:8).

You might wonder, "How do I to live 'in Jesus'? What does that mean?" Well, it works the same way as when you first accepted Him into your life. "And now, just as you accepted Christ Jesus as your Lord, you must continue to follow him" (Colossians 2:6). How did you come to accept Him? You did it by trusting Him: "And my righteous ones will live by faith" (Hebrews 10:38). You turned your life over to God, to be completely His, to serve and obey Him, and you accepted Jesus as your Savior. You couldn't bridge the gap your sins had created between you and God; you couldn't change your heart; but when you gave yourself to God, Jesus did all this for you. By faith you became His and by faith you'll grow up in Him. You grow by giving and receiving. You give your heart, your will, your service, your whole self to Him to obey everything He asks you to do. And you also need to receive all of Jesus, the One who provides every blessing. You receive Him to live in your heart, to be your strength, your goodness, your constant helper—to give you the power to obey.

It's very important to dedicate yourself to God every morning, before you do anything else. When you first wake up, pray something like this: "Take me, Lord, to be completely Yours. I give all my plans to You. Use me today to do the things You need me to do. Live with me, and work through me." If you do this every day, it will keep you on track and keep you connected to God. Every morning dedicate yourself to God for the day. Surrender all your plans to Him, to be carried out or given up as He impresses you. Day by day, you'll be giving your life into God's hands, and day by day, your life will become more and more like Christ's.

When you live with Jesus, your life will be restful. You may not feel excited all the time, but you'll always feel a peaceful trust. Your hope is not in yourself; it's in Jesus. Your weakness is connected to His strength, your ignorance to His wisdom, your finite life to His infinite greatness. Don't rely on yourself or think about your faults all the time. Instead, think about Jesus. Think about the beauty and the perfection of His character. Think how unselfish He is, how humble. Be awed by His purity and holiness and by His love which is beyond all measure. It's by loving Him, copying Him, depending completely on Him, that you'll be changed to be like Him.

Jesus says, "Remain in Me." These words carry the idea of rest, dependability, and confidence. He invites you, "Come to me... and I will give you rest" (Matthew 11:28). David said, "Be still in the presence of the LORD, and wait patiently for him to act" (Psalm 37:7). And Isaiah assures you, "In quietness and confidence is your strength" (Isaiah 30:15). You won't find this rest by sitting around doing nothing. When Jesus promises rest He combines it with a call to work: "Take my yoke upon you....and you will find rest for your souls" (Matthew 11:29). It's when your heart rests most fully on Jesus that you'll be the most dedicated to working for Him.

Staying Connected With Jesus

Thinking about Jesus will keep you connected to the source of strength and life. But when you think about yourself, you lose that connection. That's why Satan constantly works to keep your attention away from the One who saves you. He tries to prevent you from staying connected with Jesus. Satan will try every possible way to distract you: fun, busyness, problems, sadness, or other people's faults. But don't be deceived by his schemes to get you off track.

One of Satan's tricks, especially when you really want to live for God, is to get you to focus on your own faults and weaknesses. As Satan separates you from Jesus he hopes to discourage you so you'll give up. It's dangerous to focus on yourself and get stuck in worry and fear about whether you can ever be saved. All this turns you away from the Source of your strength. Hand your life over to God, and trust Him. Talk and think about Jesus. Lose your whole self in Him. Don't listen to your doubt; get rid of your fears. Say, "My old self has been crucified with Christ. It is no longer I who live, but Christ lives in me. So I live in this earthly body by trusting in the Son of God, who loved me and gave himself for me" (Galatians 2:20). Rest in God. He is able to "guard what" you "have entrusted to Him" (2 Timothy 1:12). If you will leave yourself in His hands, "overwhelming victory is [yours] through Christ, who loved [you]" (Romans 8:37).

When Jesus became human, He attached you to Himself by a love that can never be broken, except by your own choice. Satan will constantly tempt you to break this tie—to separate yourself from Jesus. You'll need to watch carefully and pray, so that nothing will persuade you to turn against Him. You're always free to do that. But keep your mind focused on Jesus and He will protect you. As long as you look to Jesus, you're safe. Nothing can pull you out of His hand. As you constantly watch Him, "the Lord—who is the Spirit—makes [you] more and more like Him as [you] are changed into His glorious image" (2 Corinthians 3:18).

That's how Jesus first followers grew to be like Him. When they heard Him speak, they felt they had to be with Him. They searched for Jesus until they found Him, and then they followed Him everywhere. They hung out with Him, ate with Him, talked with Him, and traveled with Him. They were with Him like students are with a teacher, learning all the time. They looked to Him, like servants to a master, to learn what He wanted them to do. These disciples were men "as human as we are" (James 5:17). They had the same battles with sin that we fight. They needed the same help from God in order to live holy lives.

John was one of Jesus' closest friends and he loved Jesus deeply, but at first John was not a very lovable person. He was stubborn, he didn't hesitate to step on others for his own advantage, he was impulsive, and he had serious anger issues. But as he got to know Jesus, he saw his faults and he was humbled. Every day, he watched Jesus. He saw His strength and patience, His power and tenderness, His majesty and humility; and he was filled with admiration and love. The more he saw of Jesus, the more his heart was drawn toward Him, until finally he lost sight of himself in love for his Master. He surrendered his resentful, ambitious temper to Jesus. The Holy Spirit gave him a new heart. Jesus' love changed his character. That's what will happen to you, too, when you connect with Jesus. When you turn your heart over to Jesus, He will remove the defects in your character. His Spirit will soften your heart. He'll make you humble and willing to learn, and He'll lift your thoughts and your desires toward God.

Jesus is Closer Now Than Ever

When Jesus returned to heaven, His followers could still feel His presence with them. They could still feel His love and sense His guidance. Jesus, who had walked and talked and prayed with them, spoke a final message of hope and comfort to their hearts. And then, while He was still speaking, they watched Him go up into heaven. They saw a cloud of angels welcome Him and they heard His last words, "I am with you always, even to the end of the age" (Matthew 28:20). He had returned to heaven as a human. They knew that even though Jesus now stood before the throne of God in heaven, He was still their Friend and Savior. They knew His love and care for them had not changed. He still related with their suffering. He was presenting the value of His own precious blood to God, showing His wounded hands and feet as a reminder of the price He had paid to rescue them. Jesus' disciples knew He had gone back to heaven to prepare places for them, and that He would come back and bring them home to be with Him forever (John 14:2-3).

After Jesus returned to heaven, his followers met together, eagerly bringing their requests to their Heavenly Father in the name of Jesus. In intense awe they bowed down in prayer, repeating Jesus' promise, "you will ask the Father directly, and he will grant your request because you use my name. You haven't done this before. Ask, using my name, and you will receive, and you will have abundant joy" (John 16:23, 24). Their faith grew stronger and stronger, as they claimed the powerful truth, "Christ Jesus died for us and was raised to life for us, and He is sitting in the place of honor at God's right hand, pleading for us" (Romans 8:34). Then, Jesus sent the Holy Spirit, the Comforter, to them. Jesus had said, the Holy Spirit "will be in you" (John 14:17, see Acts 2). He had also said, "it is best for you that I go away, because if I don't, the Advocate won't come. If I do go away, then I will send him to you" (John 16:7). Through the Holy Spirit, Jesus still lived in their hearts. Their connection with Him was actually closer than when He was physically with them. The light and love and power of Jesus shone out through them and everyone was amazed and "recognized them as men who had been with Jesus" (Acts 4:13).

All that Jesus was to His first followers, He wants to be to you. In His last prayer, with the little group of disciples gathered around Him, Jesus said, "I am praying not only for these disciples but also for all who will ever believe in me through their message" (John 17:20). Jesus prayed for us! How cool is that! But more than that, think about what He prayed for: He prayed for us to be united with Him, just as He is united with the Father (John 17:21). He wants to be as close to you as He is to His Father! He wants you to be just as loved as He is. He wants you to have access to all the Father gives to Him. He knows you're powerless on your own because He was powerless too when He lived here on earth. Jesus said, "The Son can do nothing by himself" (John 5:19). "My Father who lives in me does his work through me" (John 14:10). So, if Jesus is living in you, He'll work in your heart, giving you "the desire and the power to do what pleases him" (Philippians 2:13). You'll work just like He worked, and you'll show the same attitude toward others. And so, loving Him and living in Him, you'll be "growing in every way more and more like" Jesus (Ephesians 4:15).

Discussion Questions

1. How does the Bible describe the process of meeting God and growing spiritually? Luke 8:4-8

2. What causes a seed to grow? They can't cause themselves to grow, so what is their role?

3. What is the equivalent of sunlight, rain, and food for spiritual growth? John 8:12; John 4:13, 14; John 6:35

    What has helped you the most in your spiritual growth so far?

4. What is your role in your spiritual growth? John 15:1-8

5. What are some of the ways you can perform this role? John 15:9, 10; Hebrews 12:2; Psalm 143:8; Proverbs 3:5,6; Proverbs 16:3; Matthew 11:28-30

6. Which of these ideas have been most helpful to you in your spiritual journey so far? What are some examples of how you apply them?

S T E P

We made direct amends to such people whenever possible, except when to do so would injure them or others.

"Therefore, if you are offering your gift at the altar and there remember that your brother has something against you, leave your gift there in front of the altar. First go and be reconciled to your brother, then come and offer your gift."

~ Matthew 5:23-24

A Reason For Living

(The Work and the Life)

Respond to the call to love others like Jesus loves you.

G od is the source of life and light and joy to the universe. Like rays of light streaming from the sun, like water gushing from a fountain, good things pour out from God to every living creature. When you have God in your heart, you too will shower His love and blessings on others.

The Joy of Loving Others

Jesus yearns to rescue broken people. While He was on earth, He spent all His time encouraging and healing people who struggled with pain and dysfunction. But more than that, He actually gave up His life and suffered a terrible death to pay sin's ransom for us. He held nothing back in His passion to bring hope and healing to suffering people. The angels are like Jesus that way—they also love to work for the happiness of others. Some people are arrogant and proud; they think they're too good to hang out with those that don't meet their standards. But the noble angels love to serve the outcasts. Everyone in heaven has this same attitude of self-sacrificing love. That's why heaven is so full of joy. As you follow Jesus, that attitude will rub off on you, too. Because of Him, you'll start to care about other people and want to help them.

When you have Jesus' love in our heart, it will be like a sweet fragrance that can't be hidden. Everyone around you will feel its holy influence. The love of Jesus in your life is like a spring of water in the desert, bubbling up to refresh those who are dying of the thirst in their souls. You know that thirst too, don't you? You may have tried many damaging ways to satisfy your thirst before you found Jesus' love to be the Water of Life. Now you get to show your love for Jesus by working as He did to encourage and help other people. Because you love Him, you'll want to show the same love, kindness, and sympathy to others as He does to you. One of your first opportunities to do this happens when you become willing to make amends to those you have harmed. When you go to them to make amends, they will see the changes God is making in you. They will see how you treat them with a new respect and with gentle dignity. Through your behavior, they will begin to catch a glimpse of Jesus' love—the love that has been changing your heart.

Loving Isn't Easy

Jesus didn't live His life for His own interests or pleasure. Everything He did was to bless someone else. From the rough manger where He was born to the rough cross where He died, Jesus lived a life of self-denial. He worked long hours, traveled long distances on foot, served difficult people, faced difficult challenges and took on exhausting responsibilities. He said, "the Son of Man came not to be served but to serve others and to give his life as a ransom for many" (Matthew 20:28). This was the one great purpose of His life. Nothing else mattered. Doing His Father's will and finishing the work His Father had sent Him to do was the food for His soul. He gave no thought to pleasing Himself.

Now that Jesus has forgiven you, and you've received the gift of eternal life, you'll find yourself eager to share His love with others. You know He died for them, and you want them to receive His incredible gifts, too. You want to do everything possible to make the world a better place. As God continues to remove the defects from your character, He'll give you the same unselfish attitude as Jesus. Now that you've turned your life over to Jesus and He's begun to restore you to sanity, you'll find yourself wanting to tell others what a precious friend you've found in Jesus. You can't keep it to yourself! His goodness fills your heart and His Holy Spirit guides you, and you're so full of joy you can't keep quiet about it. You have experienced for yourself that God is good, and you have something to tell. One of Jesus' disciples, Philip, when he first found Jesus, immediately hurried to bring his friends to meet Jesus, too. You'll be doing that also, telling them about the amazing life you have with Jesus now. You'll want more than anything to live your life like Jesus did, helping those around you to see "the Lamb of God who takes away the sin of the world" (John 1:29).

When you work to encourage and comfort others, your own life will be encouraged and blessed, too. That's why God gave you a part in His plan to rescue hurting people. He works to remove your shortcomings and give you a character like Jesus, and as your life changes you'll bless others. There is no higher honor or greater joy that God could give you. You'll come closer to God when you love other people than by anything else you could do.

God could have asked the angels to do all the loving and serving. He could have found a way to win us back without asking us to help each other. But in His incredible love He chose to make us His co-workers. Jesus calls you to work along with Him so you can share the blessing of serving others. It won't be easy, but as you join Him in the battle to rescue people who are hurting, your heart will be joined to His. You'll become willing to put your own needs last for the good of others—just like Jesus who "was rich, yet for your sakes he became poor, so that by his poverty he could make you rich" (2 Corinthians 8:9). Being part of the action with Jesus is what really makes life worth living.

Loving Will Help You Grow

As you work with Jesus, loving people and bringing them to Him, you'll find that you need more and more of Him. You'll crave a greater knowledge of spiritual things. You'll long to be like Him. As you plead with God for help and holiness, He will strengthen your faith and you'll drink in the deep truths He reveals to you. In the challenges which will certainly come, you'll constantly turn to the Bible and prayer for help and strength. Seeking Him so earnestly while working in the trenches ministering to others will give you a rich experience of Jesus.

Working with Jesus and serving people will change you. Your character will grow deep and steady and beautiful like His, and you'll have His peace and joy. With your sights set on such lofty goals, you'll have no room for laziness or selfishness. As you exercise faith and love, you'll become strong in your work for God. You'll understand spiritual things more clearly, your faith will grow stable, and your prayers will become powerful. The Spirit of God will touch your heart to beat in tune with His. Unselfish labor for the good of others is the surest way to cooperate with God in working out your own salvation (Philippians 2:12, 13).

The only way to grow spiritually is to do the work Jesus has given you to do—doing your best to help and encourage others. Strength comes by exercise; activity is essential to life. Some people live a very passive Christian life, accepting God's blessings and yet doing nothing for Him. That's like someone who eats and never exercises. Doing that will eventually kill you! And it's just as true spiritually as it is physically. If you refuse to move your arms and legs, soon you won't be able to use them. And if you don't use the spiritual abilities God gives you, your character won't grow and you'll lose any strength you had to begin with.

You're Called to Work With Jesus

God chose you to be His helper in saving people. He calls you to share with other people the awesome fact that He is crazy about them and that He delights in their recovery. Every person God rescues He calls to join Him in the work of rescuing others. He asks all His followers to use their own talents and the opportunities at hand to obey His call, "go and make disciples of all the nations" (Matthew 28:19). Because of God's love for you while you were lost in your own junk, you owe a debt to those who are still lost to bring them to Him for help. God rescued you, not just for your own benefit, but so you could help rescue others.

If all those Jesus has saved responded to His call, there would be thousands working to rescue people from their addictions and dysfunction where today there are only a few. You don't need to travel far away or do anything heroic, in order to work for Jesus. You'll find people who desperately need Him everywhere you go including your own home, your workplace, and even your church. Jesus spent most of His life on earth working patiently in His carpenter's shop in Nazareth. No one realized who He really was, but they felt His love for them and His interest in their needs. He was as faithfully fulfilling His mission while working at His ordinary, day-to-day job as He was when He healed the sick or walked on the storm-tossed waves of the Sea of Galilee. The same is true for you. No matter how insignificant you feel, you can walk and work with Jesus.

Paul, the apostle, said, "Each of you, dear brothers and sisters, should remain as you were when God first called you" (1 Corinthians 7:24). Don't feel that you must change your occupation to work for Jesus. Whatever your line of work, you can honor your heavenly Boss by being honest and dependable and treating others well. As a true follower of Jesus, everything you do will help others to feel His love and be attracted to Him.

Do What You Can

Many Christians excuse themselves from serving God because they feel others have better talents and skills than they do. Many think that only those who are especially talented need to dedicate their abilities to God's service. Some even believe that God plays favorites and only gives such abilities to certain people. They can't believe that God has asked less talented people to join in the work or to share its rewards. But Jesus didn't present it that way. He said God calls every person to a particular task and He equips them to do that work (Matthew 25:14-30).

When you have a loving attitude, you can do even the smallest or least important job "as though you were working for the Lord" (Colossians 3:23). When you love God, your life will show it. The sweet fragrance of Jesus will surround you, and your influence will inspire and encourage others. Don't wait for great opportunities or to acquire special abilities before you go to work for God. Don't worry what anyone thinks of you. If your faith is sincere and people see that you want the best for them, your efforts won't be lost.

Even if you're the most humble and poorest of Jesus' followers, you can encourage and help others. You might not realize that you're doing anything special, but your influence can start waves of blessing that will spread wide and deep. You may never know how much good you have caused until the day when Jesus returns and says, "Well done!" You don't need to stress about making a difference. Just live each day, faithfully doing whatever God asks at the moment and your life won't be a waste of time. Your own character will be growing more and more like Jesus' character. As you work with Him in this life, you're preparing for a higher work when you'll be with Him face-to-face in the life to come.

Discussion Questions

1. What does a healthy, growing plant or tree do naturally? Matthew 7:16, 17

2. What does Jesus say His followers will do? John 15:4-11

3. When you were still lost in your craziness, pain, or addictions, what kind of "fruit" did you produce?

4. Now that you have met Jesus and He has begun to heal you, what kind of fruit will He produce in you? Galatians 5:22; Ephesians 5:8-10

    What changes have you see in yourself that give you hope?

5. Jesus told little short stories called parables to teach lessons. Here are two of them: Mark 4:26-32. In both of these stories, Jesus is telling you something about how your healing will happen and what you will do as you continue to grow in your recovery and in Him. What do you hear Him saying to you?

6. Notice how Samuel encouraged and supported to his struggling friends and family:

> *God will never abandon you, because He wants you to know He's not like that; because He delights for you to become His family. It would cause deep wounds if I harm God by not praying for you. I will show you the good ways that will make your life sweet. Think about the huge things God has done for you and give your whole self to Him. Don't keep hurting yourself, breaking yourself down, or you will destroy yourself.*
>
> *1 Samuel 12:22-24 (paraphrase)*

If you follow Samuel's example, what will you do for the people you love who are struggling?

STEP 10

We continued to take personal inventory, and when we were wrong, promptly admitted it.

"So if you think you are standing firm, be careful that you don't fall."

~ *1 Corinthians 10:12*

10

Give Me More!
(A Knowledge of God)

The more you know and trust God, the better He can help you to heal.

God uses every possible way to communicate with you. He's eager for you to know Him well and to trust Him to help you with each step of your recovery. Without His help, you'll struggle to stay on track. Continued recovery depends on carefully monitoring your feelings, thoughts, and actions. As you continue to take personal inventory each day, God will help you to see when you get off track, and to admit it quickly before things get out of control again. The better you know Him, the more you'll love and trust Him, the more clearly you'll recognize His prompting, and the more He can help you.

Knowing God through nature

One of the ways God makes Himself known to you is through nature. The wonders of the natural world speak constantly, telling you of the love and magnificence of God. You can hear God's voice through His creations.

The green fields, the tall trees, the buds and flowers, the passing clouds, the falling rain, the rippling brook, and the beauty of the night sky speak to your heart and invite you to get to know the One who made them all.

Jesus used things in nature as subjects for many of the lessons He taught. He said the birds don't worry about what to eat because God feeds them, and the flowers don't worry about what to wear because God clothes them. Jesus made His lessons memorable by tying them to the familiar things of nature. Two thousand years later, you can't help but remember those lessons when you see a bird or a beautiful flower.

God wants His children to appreciate His creations and to delight in the simple, quiet beauty of our earthly home. He loves beauty—especially beauty of character. He wants you to develop purity and simplicity like the natural loveliness of the flowers.

If you stop to listen, nature will teach you important lessons of obedience and trust. From the ancient stars that follow their appointed paths through unlimited space, to the miniscule atom, all nature obeys the Creator's commands. God cares for everything and sustains everything He created. The One who cares for all the unnumbered worlds in the vast universe also cares for the needs of the little brown sparrow that sings its humble song without fear. When people go about their daily work, and when they pray; when they lie down at night, and when they wake up in the morning; when the wealthy feast in their elegant homes, or when the poor feed their children a scanty meal; God tenderly watches each one. God notices every tear and every smile.

When you fully believe this, you'll stop worrying. You won't feel disappointed so often because you'll leave everything, big or small, to God's care. God is not surprised or confused by your problems, and He's not overwhelmed by the difficulties. Trusting in God's care will bring you peace in the chaotic storms of life and hope for the wonderful future He's preparing for you.

Our earth, even after centuries of sin and destruction, is still stunningly beautiful. Like a jewel spinning through space, it's filled with mystery and majesty. As your senses delight in the wonders of the earth, think what the new earth will be like after God restores it to its original perfection. Our new home will never experience the misery of sin or addiction or death. Nature will no longer live under the curse of sin. The home God is preparing for us will be more amazing than you can possibly imagine. The beautiful gifts God gave us in nature reveal only the tiniest glimpse of His glory. The Bible says, "No eye has seen, no ear has heard, and no mind has imagined what God has prepared for those who love Him" (1 Corinthians 2:9).

The poet and the biologist can say many things about nature, but it's the one who knows God who appreciates the earth's beauty the most, because he recognizes his Father's creativity and skill and sees God's love in every flower, shrub, and tree. Only those who see God's love letter to us in the hills and valleys, rivers and seas, will fully appreciate their significance. They are all expressions of His love.

Knowing God through the Holy Spirit's influence

God speaks to you through events in your life and through the influence of His Spirit on your thoughts and feelings. If your heart is open to God's leading you can find valuable lessons in your circumstances and in the daily changes taking place around you. Speaking of God's leading in the past, David, the psalmist, says, "The unfailing love of the Lord fills the earth" (Psalm 33:5); "Those who are wise will take all this to heart; they will see in our history the faithful love of the Lord" (Psalm 107:43).

Knowing God through the Bible

God also speaks to you through the Bible. In its pages you can see a clearer picture of His character, of His relationships with people, and of His great work in saving sinners. The Bible tells the history of ordinary people just like you. Even the most notable of these characters—like Adam, Noah, and Moses—were people "as human as we are" (James 5:17). In the Scriptures, you can see how they struggled through discouragements like yours, how they gave into temptation just like you've done, and how they took courage to stand up again and conquer with God's help. Their lives will encourage you in your quest to live your life God's way. As you read about their adventures with God, of the way He loved them and blessed them, and of the work they did through His power, you'll be encouraged to trust God like they did. The same Spirit that inspired them will inspire you to be like them and to walk with God as they did.

Jesus said, "the Scriptures point to me!" (John 5:39). The whole Bible, Old and New Testaments, tells of Jesus, the Savior, who is our hope of eternal life. From the first record of creation—for "nothing was created except through Him" (John 1:3)—to the closing promise, "Look, I am coming soon" (Revelation 22:12), you can read of His works and listen to His voice. If you want to know Jesus, study the Holy Bible. Fill your whole heart with the words of God. They are the living water, satisfying your burning thirst. They are the living bread from heaven. Jesus declares, "unless you eat the flesh of the Son of Man and drink his blood, you cannot have eternal life within you" (John 6:53). And He explained what He meant, "the very words I have spoken to you are spirit and life" (John 6:63). In the natural world, your body develops from what you eat and drink. It's the same in the spiritual world— what you feed your mind shapes your soul.

Even the angels eagerly seek to understand God's work to rescue us, and we ourselves will study the story with awe and wonder in heaven. We'll be forever discovering more about our Redeemer. Doesn't that make it worth studying now? The immeasurable love and sacrifice of Jesus—nothing matters more! Think about the One who rescued you, and who pleads on your behalf, and you'll trust Him more and more. When you consider that God's entire focus since sin invaded this planet has been to save His people from their sins, you can't help but love Him. The more you think about these things, the more your love and faith in Him will grow and the more your prayers will be in tune with God's heart. Every day you'll see more evidence that He is able to bring you to full and permanent recovery (Hebrews 7:25).

As you think about Jesus' perfect character, you'll want to be totally changed and remade to be as pure and good as He is. You'll hunger and thirst to become like Jesus because you adore Him. The more you focus on Jesus, the more you'll talk of Him to the people around you and the more careful you'll be to honor Him before others.

How to get the most from studying the Bible

The Bible wasn't written only for professionals and highly educated people. Quite the opposite; it was written for ordinary people. It makes perfectly clear the things you need to know to be save. Only those who follow their own opinions rather than the plain truth of the Bible are at risk of being lost.

It's not a good idea to just accept the opinion of another person about what the Bible teaches; you need to study the words of God for yourself. If you allow other people to do your thinking for you, your mind will become weak, and it will be hard for you to tell what's true. Your mind will become weak if you don't exercise it by concentrating on ideas that matter. You'll lose your ability to understand the Bible. But if you study hard and seek to understand the Bible, comparing one scripture to another, your mind will grow strong. In fact, nothing will strengthen your mind more than studying the Bible. No other book has such power to inspire great thoughts as the ennobling truths of the Bible. If you study God's Word you'll think more deeply, you'll be respected for your excellent character, and you'll have a rock-solid purpose in life—something few people have.

Don't read the Bible in a hurry. If you rush through it, you might read the whole Bible and still miss its beauty and fail to understand its deep and hidden meaning. Study a verse until you really understand what it means and what God is saying to you. A slower study like this is more valuable than skimming many chapters and getting nothing out of them. Keep your Bible with you. Each time you have an opportunity, read it. Memorize verses. Wherever you are, whenever you can, read a few verses and think about the message until it sticks in your mind.

Wisdom comes when you pay close attention and pray over the words. Some parts of the Bible are so clear you can't miss them, but other verses require closer study. Compare one Bible verse to another to get a broader perspective. Study carefully, pray, and think. Studying like this will really pay off. It's like a miner who discovers veins of precious metal hidden beneath the earth's surface. If you search the Word of God you'll find rich treasure. If you look for the truth without giving up, digging for it like for buried treasure, you'll find what the careless reader misses. Ponder God's words and they will refresh your mind like streams flowing from the fountain of life.

Always pray before studying the Bible. Ask the Holy Spirit to explain it to you, and He will. When Nathanael came to Jesus, the Savior exclaimed, "Now here is a genuine son of Israel—a man of complete integrity." Nathanael asked, "How do you know about me?" Jesus replied, "I could see you under the fig tree before Philip found you" (John 1:47, 48). Jesus will see you also in your secret place of prayer. He'll hear when you ask Him to help you understand the truth. Angels from heaven will be with you when you humbly ask for God's guidance.

The Holy Spirit honors Jesus. It's His job to help you see Jesus. He'll show you Jesus' perfect goodness. He'll assure you of Jesus' great power to rescue you from your addictions. Jesus said, "[The Spirit] will bring me glory by telling you whatever He receives from me" (John 16:14). The Holy Spirit, the Spirit of truth, is the only One who can introduce you to God. Just think how much God values and loves us: He gave His Son to die for us, and He gives His Spirit to be our teacher and constant guide!

Discussion Questions

1. God wants you to know Him so you feel safe to trust Him. Here are some ways He speaks:

    Nature. What do you see in God's creations and His care of them that speaks to you of Him? What do you hear Him say to you?

    Circumstances. What experience have you had where you could clearly see God working in your life, even if not until after the fact? How does this help you trust Him?

    Holy Spirit. When have you sensed God's Spirit impressing you about something, or answering a question you have asked Him, or guiding you in some way?

2. What will help you understand the Bible and hear God speak to you?

    Luke 11:13   _____

    Acts 17:11   _____

    Hebrews 3:13   _____

    Mark 1:35   _____

    Psalm 25:5   _____

    Which of these have you already tried? How has it helped you? Which do you feel you need to do more?

3. The most amazing way God communicates with us is through
    Jesus. God so wants us to know Him that He sent His Son
    to actually became one of us—a human—Jesus, so that we
    could see what He is really like. What does the Bible say
    about this? Hebrews 1:1, 2; John 14:8, 9

4. But the Bible doesn't just tell you <u>about</u> Jesus. Jesus actually
    speaks to you through the Bible. Here are a few of the things
    He says:

    Jeremiah 31:3   _____

    Isaiah 1:18   _____

    Jeremiah 29:11   _____

    Deuteronomy 31:6   _____

    John 6:35   _____

    John 6:37-40   _____

    John 14:1-3   _____

    How is your heart responding right now to these messages
    from Jesus?

S T11E P

We sought through prayer and meditation to improve our conscious contact with God, praying only for knowledge of His will for us and the power to carry it out.

"Let the word of Christ dwell in you richly."

~ Colossians 3:16

CHAPTER 11

The Privilege of Prayer
(Talking With God)

Stay in touch with the One who is healing you.

God speaks to you through nature and the Bible. He speaks through His work in your life. And He speaks through the influence of His Spirit. But it is not enough for you to just listen when God speaks; you need also to share your heart with Him. In order to be spiritually alive and growing, you need to be connected with your heavenly Father. You may think about Him, you may admire what He's done, you may even be thankful for His kindness and blessings, but you can do all that and never really connect with Him. Real connection happens when you tell Him about your life and what's going on with you.

Pray Because You Need To

Prayer is opening your heart to God like you would to a friend. It's not that He needs you to tell Him. He already knows, and He's crazy about you, after all! But telling Him helps you to connect with Him. Prayer doesn't bring God down to you, it brings you up to Him. When Jesus was on earth, He taught His disciples how to pray. He told them to turn over all their "worries and cares to God" (1 Peter 5:7). He promised God would hear, and you can be sure He will hear you too.

Jesus prayed a lot. Because He was human, He could fully relate to our needs and weaknesses. He needed God's help every day to handle the responsibilities and challenges He faced. Jesus is your example in everything. He knows what it's like to feel weak "for He faced all of the same testings we do, yet He did not sin" (Hebrews 4:15). He was different than you only in that He was sinless—everything in Him hated evil. Because of that, He suffered an anguish when surrounded by sin that none of us will ever know. In the weakness of His humanity, this torment made prayer necessary for His survival. Talking with His Father brought comfort to His heart and gave Him joy. If Jesus, the Son of God, felt the need to pray constantly, how much more do you?

Your heavenly Father is just waiting to pour out blessings on you! You can drink in His love like someone dying of thirst who plunges into a great fountain of water. It makes no sense to pray so little, especially when God is ready and willing to hear the faintest cry from even the most hopeless person. Don't hesitate to tell God what you need. Don't struggle alone with your temptations, when God longs to help you. He's ready to give you more than you could ever ask or dream. Pray much! Trust much! The angels love to bow before God; they love to be near Him. They consider talking with God their greatest joy. And you, who so desperately need His help, can know that same joy when you come to Him in prayer.

Spiritual and emotional darkness will close around you if you don't bother to pray. The enemy will whisper temptations and draw you to sin and then he will trap you. But he can only do that if you don't take time to pray and to take advantage of the help God is ready to give you. Remember that prayer is the key in the hand of faith that unlocks heaven's storehouse, where God holds unlimited resources to help you. Without constantly praying and keeping all your problems and concerns before Him, you're in danger of becoming careless, of getting off track, and returning to your addiction. Satan and his evil angels try constantly to stop you from praying so you won't receive help to resist temptation. Don't let them! Keep praying.

Conditions For Answers to Prayer

How can you be sure God will hear and answer your prayers? There are a few conditions. The first is that you feel your need for Him. God promised, "I will pour out water to quench your thirst" (Isaiah 44:3). It's when you're thirsty for God's goodness, when you really want Him in your life, that you can be sure you'll have Him. Until you're willing to accept the Holy Spirit's influence, your heart won't be ready to receive God's blessings. Even though God sees your needs and problems and deeply cares about them, He still urges you to ask Him for what you need. Asking helps you to recognize your need. He says, "Keep on asking, and you will receive what you ask for" (Matthew 7:7). And "since He did not spare even His own Son but gave Him up for us all, won't He also give us everything else?" (Romans 8:32).

Repentance is another condition for preparing your heart to receive God's answer to your prayers. If you secretly keep doing wrong, or even wishing you could, if you hang on to your sin, God won't answer your prayer. But God will always eagerly accept your prayer when you're sorry for your sins. When you've tried to make amends, you can be sure God will answer. Please understand that it's not your good behavior that brings God's favor. It's Jesus' perfect life that saves you and His death that makes you right with God. But you do have a part to play in meeting the conditions of answered prayer.

The next condition for answered prayer is faith. "Anyone who wants to come to Him must believe that God exists and that He rewards those who sincerely seek Him" (Hebrews 11:6). Jesus said, "you can pray for anything, and if you believe that you've received it, it will be yours" (Mark 11:24). Do you believe Him? The promise is unlimited, and the One who promised is faithful. When you don't receive the things you ask for, at the time you ask, keep believing that the Lord hears and that He will answer. It's possible that what you requested isn't in your best interest. Your Father loves you too much to give you something that will hurt you. You can be sure that He will give you the very thing you yourself would want if you could see all the facts like He does. When God doesn't seem to answer your prayers, hang on to His promise. His answer will come, and you'll get what you need most. But don't assume your prayers will always be answered exactly the way you think they should be. God is too wise to make mistakes, and too good to hold back any good thing from His children (Psalm 84:11). So trust Him, even when you don't see the answer to your prayers right away.

You can count on God's promise, "Keep on asking, and you will receive what you ask for" (Matthew 7:7). If you let your doubts and fears control you, or if you try to come up with your own solution, your confusion and problems will only get worse. But if you come to God, feeling helpless and dependent as you really are, and in humble, trusting faith tell Him what you need, He will listen and answer your cry. God knows all, sees all, and is more than able to help you. Prayer will connect you with Him. You might not be able to tell, but you can be sure that Jesus is bending over in compassion and love. You may not see Him or feel Him, but He is right there with you.

When you come to God asking for forgiveness and help, come with a spirit of love and forgiveness in your own heart. It's not reasonable to pray, "and forgive us our sins, as we have forgiven those who sin against us" if you aren't actually willing to forgive (Matthew 6:12). You can only expect God to hear your prayers to the extent you forgive others.

Persistence is another condition of answered prayer. If you want to grow spiritually, pray persistently. Keep on praying; "devote [yourself] to prayer with an alert mind and a thankful heart" (Romans 12:12; Colossians 4:2). Be "earnest and disciplined in your prayers" (1 Peter 4:7). Pray "about everything. Tell God what you need, and thank him for all he has done" (Philippians 4:6). "But you, dear friends, ...pray in the power of the Holy Spirit...and keep yourselves safe in God's love" (Jude 20, 21). Unceasing prayer is the unbroken connection of your thoughts with God. Life from God flows into your life, and from your life, purity and holiness flow back to God. Don't be lazy in prayer. Don't let anything stop you. Do everything you can to keep communicating with Jesus. Take every chance to go where prayer will happen. If you really want spiritual connection with God, attend prayer meetings or prayer groups; take every opportunity to be where you can get encouragement from heaven. And pray together as a family at home.

One-on-one With God

Above all else, don't neglect your prayer time alone, because this is the life of your soul. Spiritual health is only possible when you remember to pray. Family or public prayer, alone, is not enough. In quiet times when you're alone, open your heart to God. He sees and accepts you just the way you are. Private prayer is only for God to hear. Don't let others hear the burdens you bring to God. Find a place where you can get away from all the distractions and be alone with Him. There you can pray calmly, with your whole heart reaching out to God. And God, who sees you in that quiet place, who listens for the prayers you whisper to Him, will speak gently to your soul. By calm, simple faith you can talk with God and gain strength and endurance for the battle with Satan. God is your tower of strength.

Pray when you're alone, but also as you go about your day. In Bible times, the priests used to offer sweet incense on the alter in the temple. The fragrant smoke symbolized the prayers of the people going up to God. Throughout the day you can leave a sweet trail of prayers. Satan can't overcome you when your heart is focused on God like that. You can pray any time and any place. Nothing can stop you from turning to God in prayer. Driving down the road, surrounded by a crowd, or in the middle of a business meeting, you can talk to God about anything and seek His guidance. You can pray silently wherever you are. Keep the door of your heart wide open and give Jesus a standing invitation to come in.

You may be surrounded by a toxic, sinful environment, but you don't have to breathe in its poison. You can live above it all and breath in the pure air of heaven. You can close every door to impure thoughts and fantasies by lifting your mind to God through prayer. When you open your heart to God, you'll walk in a sacred space and have constant contact with Him.

You need to clearly see the magnificence of Jesus and really grasp the big picture of God's eternal plans for us. You need to be filled with awe at the beauty of His holiness. Ask Him to show you these things. Ask Him for a glimpse of what it will be like to live in heaven with Him. You can stay so close to God that every time a problem comes up your thoughts will turn to Him as naturally as a flower turns to the sun.

Keep your needs, your joys, your sorrows, your worries, and your fears before God. You can't trouble Him. You can't bore Him. He's never tired of hearing from you. He knows even the number of hairs on your head! He cares deeply about the needs and wishes of His children. "The Lord is full of tenderness and mercy" (James 5:11). His heart of love is touched by your cries to Him. Take everything that confuses you to God. Nothing is too big for Him to handle. He holds the world in the palm of His hand! He rules over all the business of the universe. Nothing that makes you unhappy or disturbs your peace is too small for Him to notice. There's no chapter in your life too dark for Him to read. There's no problem too difficult for Him to fix. He sees the tragedies of every person. No one is insignificant or unworthy in His eyes. When you're worried, He knows it. When something makes you happy, He's glad. He hears every heartfelt prayer you whisper. Your heavenly Father takes immediate interest in all of these things. "He heals the brokenhearted and bandages their wounds" (Psalm 147:3). The relationship between God and each of us is as unique and special as if you were the only person on earth. It's as if Jesus died for only you.

Prayer and Care

Jesus said, "Then you will ask in my name. I'm not saying I will ask the Father on your behalf for the Father himself loves you dearly." "I chose you.... so that the Father will give you whatever you ask for, using my name" (John 16:26, 27; 15:16). Praying in the name of Jesus means more than just mentioning His name at the beginning or end of a prayer. It means praying with the same attitude as Jesus has, believing His promises, depending on Him, and working the way He works.

God doesn't want you to hide away like a hermit, separating yourself from the world so that you can devote yourself to worship. He wants you to do like Jesus did. Jesus prayed alone on the mountain and then He came down to serve the people. If you don't do anything but pray you'll soon stop praying. Either that, or your prayers will become a boring habit. If you avoid people and aren't interested in their concerns, you won't have much to pray about. If you stop working for Jesus, who works so hard for you, you'll lose the whole reason for prayer. Your prayers will become self-focused. You won't think to pray for the needs of other people or for strength to help in God's mission to rescue them.

You'll lose a lot if you don't make it a priority to meet with other Christians to encourage each other in God's work. The Bible won't be as clear or as important to you. You'll begin to feel numb to its message. It won't speak to you or inspire you anymore and you won't care about spiritual things. You'll stop caring about other people. If you isolate yourself, you aren't doing what God designed you to do. Being with people causes you to care about them, and caring about them is the best possible preparation for serving them. If you talk with other Christians about God's love and His work to restore all of us, you'll be encouraged and you'll encourage others. Learn more about Jesus every day. Go to Him and get a fresh taste of His kindness. Then you'll want to talk about Him, and as you do your own heart will be warmed and encouraged. Think and talk more about Jesus, and less about yourself, and you'll have far more of His presence.

Gratitude and Praise

If you think about God every time you see a reminder of His love, you'll be thinking about Him constantly and you'll delight to talk about Him. You talk about other things because they interest you. You talk about your friends because you love them and your heart is wrapped up with them. You have even more reasons to love God. When you fall in love with Him, it will be the most natural thing in the world to make Him first in all your thoughts, and to tell people about the One you love. The rich gifts He's given weren't supposed to distract you so much that you forget Him. They're supposed to constantly remind you of Him, and to draw you to Him in love and thankfulness. Tear your mind away from the things of this world and think, instead, of Jesus who is working to rescue you so you can be with Him in Heaven.

Praise God "for His great love and for the wonderful things He has done" (Psalm 107:8). Worshipping Him is more than just asking for things. It's also thanking Him. God is kind to us in more ways than we can count, so thank Him and praise Him for what He has done.

Long ago in ancient Israel, God told His people that when they met together for His service, "there you and your families will feast in the presence of the Lord your God, and you will rejoice in all you have accomplished because the Lord your God has blessed you" (Deuteronomy 12:7). In all you do to honor God, do it with joy. Sing thank-you songs to Him! Our God is a gentle, kind Father. Never think that serving Him is supposed to make you sad or unhappy. Take pleasure in helping His cause in any way you can. Jesus bought your freedom with His life, and He doesn't want you to act as if He's cruel and demanding. He's your best friend; and when you worship Him, know that He wants to be with you and give you everything good.

God wants you to enjoy being with Him and not to find it a burden. He wants to fill your mind with His love so that warm thoughts of Him will keep popping up throughout the day. From your time alone with Him, He wants to give you strength to be honest and faithful in everything you do.

Every day, focus your thoughts on what Jesus did for you when He died on the cross. Think about Jesus until He becomes your greatest joy. Remember every blessing God gives you, remember His great love, and trust everything to the hand that was nailed to the cross for you. Join the angels in singing songs to honor our awesome God.

Discussion Questions

1. Prayer is just talking to God like you would to a friend, but this Friend is crazy about you and cares about everything that touches you. What does He tell you about coming to Him? Matthew 6:7-9; Isaiah 65:24; John 14:14; Ephesians 3:20

    How does this make you want to respond to Him?

2. If God knows your needs and feels like that about you, do you need to persuade Him to help you? If not, why do you need to pray? Which of these reasons means the most to you personally?

    a. Jeremiah 29:13   _____

    b. James 4:7   _____

    c. Proverbs 3:6   _____

    d. Matthew 5:6   _____

    e. Psalm 147:3   _____

    f. Psalm 18:2   _____

    g. Romans 15:13 _____

    h. Mark 9:24   _____

    i. 1 John 1:9   _____

    j. James 1:5   _____

3. The conditions for God to answer our prayers are shown below.

    a. Feel your need
    b. Ask
    c. Surrender
    d. Trust Him
    e. Love and forgive others
    f. Keep going to Him
    g. Pray in Jesus' name—with His thoughts and attitude

Which of these do you most need to address?

What prevents you from doing that?

What will you do to remove that barrier this week?

4. Tell about a time God answered your prayers.

S T E P

12

Having had a spiritual experience as a result of these steps, we tried to carry this message to others and to practice these principles in all our affairs.

"Brothers, if someone is caught in a sin, you who are spiritual should restore him gently. But watch yourself, or you also may be tempted."

~ Galatians 6:1

12

What to Do With Doubt
(Unanswered Questions)

How to be sure about God so you can truly celebrate life in recovery.

ave you ever struggled with doubt? Have you ever wondered if God is real, or questioned whether we're just accidents of evolution? Have you ever wondered if what the Bible says is true? If so, you're not alone. Many people, especially new Christians, are troubled with skepticism. When you read the Bible, there may be things you can't understand at first. Satan will try to use these questions to shake your faith in the Bible as God's message. Maybe you're asking, "How will I know the right way? How can I be sure about God and the Bible?" Resolving these questions is important because God and His word are the foundation of your recovery. Your confidence in them is what will enable you to carry a message of hope and healing to others.

Evidence, Not Proof

God never asks us to believe without giving us enough evidence on which to base our faith. His existence, His character, and the truthfulness of the Bible are all founded on evidence that appeals to our reason. But God has never taken away room for doubt. Our faith must rests evidence, not absolute proof. Those who wish to doubt certainly can, while those who really want to know the truth will find plenty of evidence on which to base their faith.

It's impossible for our limited minds to completely understand the character or the actions of the unlimited God. God will always be a mystery to even the most intelligent and highly educated person. "Can you solve the mysteries of God? Can you discover everything about the Almighty? Such knowledge is higher than the heavens—and who are you? It is deeper than the underworld—what do you know?" (Job 11:7, 8). The apostle Paul exclaims, "Oh, how great are God's riches and wisdom and knowledge! How impossible it is for us to understand His decisions and His ways!" (Romans 11:33).

But even though "dark clouds surround Him," we're not left without a basis for belief (Psalm 97:2). We can understand enough about God's interaction with us, and the reasons behind His actions, to glimpse a love without boundaries and a kindness blended with mind-boggling power. We can understand as much of His purpose as it is good for us to know. But beyond that, we must simply trust His great power and His great loving heart.

Mysteries of the Bible

The Bible contains mysteries as deep as the character of its Author: how sin entered our world, how God became a tiny human baby, how a soul is reborn, how the dead can be made alive, and many other subjects. But even though these mysteries are too much for the human mind to fully understand, we have no reason to doubt God or His word.

In the natural world, we're constantly surrounded with things we don't understand. The simplest forms of life present complexities that the wisest scientists can't explain. Wonders beyond our knowledge are everywhere, so why are we surprised to find mysteries in the spiritual world we can't fully understand?

God has given us enough evidence in the Bible to show that it's a gift directly from Him. Don't let the things you don't yet understand cause you to doubt His word. The apostle Peter says that in Scripture there are "some comments...hard to understand, and those who are ignorant and unstable have twisted [them]...to mean something quite different.... and this will result in their destruction" (2 Peter 3:16).

Skeptics have argued that certain unanswered questions about the Bible are reasons to doubt its credibility. But the opposite is actually true: the challenges provide strong evidence for divine inspiration. If the Bible said things about God that we could easily understand, if His greatness and majesty could be grasped with no effort, then the Bible would not be so obviously the work of God. The grandeur and mystery of the topics and ideas within its pages inspire faith in it as God's word.

The Bible reveals truth simply, adapting well to the needs and longings of the human heart. It surprises and charms the most highly educated minds, and it brings joy and healing even to those who have little or no education. And yet these simply-told truths deal with subjects so inspiring, so infinitely beyond the power of human understanding, that we can accept them only because God has said them. The Bible describes God's plan to rescue us so clearly that every person can understand the simple steps of repenting, turning back to God, and trusting in Jesus. But while the steps and the basic facts are clear, there are mysteries about why and how it all works that hint at the greatness and glory of God. The more you search the Bible, the more confident you'll be that it is the word of God. You will be awed by the magnificence of God reflected there.

When we admit that we can't fully understand the great truths of the Bible, we're admitting that our human minds can't comprehend God's superior mind. With our limited, human knowledge, we can't understand the purposes of the infinitely wise God.

Because they can't understand all its mysteries, skeptics and unbelievers reject the Bible. And even those who claim to believe it are at risk of doubt. The Bible says, "Be careful then, dear brothers and sisters. Make sure that your own hearts are not evil and unbelieving, turning you away from the living God" (Hebrews 3:12). It's right to carefully study what the Bible teaches and to search into "God's deep secrets," so far as they're revealed in Scripture (1 Corinthians 2:10). While "the Lord our God has secrets known to no one," "we and our children are accountable forever for all that He has revealed to us" (Deuteronomy 29:29).

But Satan works to twist our reasoning. Some people let their pride get in the way and feel frustrated if they can't figure everything out. They can't admit their limitations and they aren't willing to wait patiently until God is ready to reveal the truth to them. They feel they should be able to understand the Bible by their own wisdom without help from God, and because they can't, they deny its authority.

There are many popular theories and beliefs which people assume to have come from the Bible but, in fact, have no support from the Bible at all and even oppose its teachings. These things have caused a lot of doubt and confusion. But the problem is not with the Bible; the problem is with people's interpretation of it.

The Unlimited Treasures of Knowledge

If it were possible for humans to fully understand God and all He does, what would happen after achieving that goal? There would be no further discovery of truth, no growth in knowledge, no further development of our minds or hearts. God would no longer be supreme. People would stop growing spiritually because they would have learned all there is to know. Thank God this isn't true. God is unlimited. In Him are "hidden all the treasures of wisdom and knowledge" (Colossians 2:3). Throughout eternity people will continue searching and learning about God, and yet they will never learn all there is to know about His wisdom, His goodness, and His power.

God intends for you to continually discover more and more of the profound truths in the Bible. Such deep understanding comes only in one way: through the help of His Holy Spirit, the One who gave the message. "[No] one can know God's thoughts except God's own Spirit" (1 Corinthians 2:11, 10). Jesus promised, "when the Spirit of truth comes, He will guide you into all truth. He will not speak on His own but will tell you what He has heard. He will tell you about the future" (John 16:13, 14).

Causes of Doubt

God wants you to think for yourself. Studying the Bible will strengthen your mind and lift up your thoughts like nothing else can. But be careful not to trust your own reason more than you trust God. Sin has degraded our minds so much that we are at risk of misunderstanding. Trust God to teach you, ask for the Holy Spirit to help you, and you'll gain insight you couldn't get any other way. The more you see of God's power and wisdom, the more awe you will feel as you seek Him in His word.

There are many things in the Bible that may seem hard to understand, but God will make them clear if you ask for His help. Without the Holy Spirit's guidance, we're constantly in danger of twisting the meaning of Bible verses or of hearing what we want to hear. Reading the Bible can mess you up if you open it without reverence or prayer. If you aren't really seeking God or His will, your mind may be clouded with doubt, and studying the Bible may actually make you more skeptical. Satan can take control of your thoughts and suggest interpretations that are wrong. If a person isn't trying to follow God, then no matter how educated they are, they're likely to make mistakes in understanding the Bible. It's not safe to trust their explanations. Those who read the Bible to find inconsistencies or mistakes don't have spiritual insight. They'll see many reasons to doubt things that are really quite plain and simple.

People may not want to admit it, but the real reason they doubt God is that they don't like the restrictions or teachings of the Bible. Since they don't want to do what the Bible says, they're ready to doubt that it comes from God. You'll know the truth when you really want to know the truth and when you're willing to obey it. If you come to the Bible with that attitude, you'll find plenty of evidence that it is God's word, and God will give you wisdom to understand it.

Jesus said, "Anyone who wants to do the will of God will know whether my teaching is from God or is merely my own" (John 7:17). Instead of questioning what you don't understand, apply what you do understand and God will help you sort out the things that still confuse you.

The Evidence of Personal Experience

There is one evidence everyone can grasp—from the most educated to those who can't even read—and that is the evidence of personal experience. God encourages us to prove for ourselves that His word is real and His promises are true. He invites us to "taste and see that the Lord is good" (Psalm 34:8). Instead of trusting what other people say, experience God's promises for yourself. He says, "Ask, using my name, and you will receive" (John 16:24). He keeps His promises. They've never failed; they never can fail. As you draw close to Jesus, rejoicing in His love, your doubt and darkness will disappear in the light of His presence.

The apostle Paul said God "has rescued us from the kingdom of darkness and transferred us into the Kingdom of his dear Son" (Colossians 1:13). And everyone who has been rescued from death knows "that God is true" (John 3:33). You can say without any doubt, "I needed help, and Jesus helped me. I longed to be with Him and He came to me. He gave me everything I needed. Why do I believe in Jesus? Because He rescued me from the things that were ruining my life. Why do I believe the Bible? Because through it I've heard Him speak to my soul."

You Can Be Sure

You can know for sure that the Bible is true and that Jesus is the Son of God. You can know that you're not "making clever stories" (2 Peter 1:16). You can "grow in the grace and knowledge of our Lord and Savior Jesus

Christ" (2 Peter 3:18). As you grow, God will continue to give you clearer understanding of the Bible. You'll see new insights and beauty in its sacred truths. This has been true throughout the history of God's people and it will be true to the end. "The way of the righteous is like the first gleam of dawn, which shines ever brighter until the full light of day" (Proverbs 4:18).

You can trust this promise! In heaven, your abilities will join with God's strength and your powers will be brought into direct contact with God, the Source of all wisdom. Just think! All the things God has done which have confused you in the past will be made clear. God will explain the things you didn't understand on earth. Where your limited mind was confused, where it seemed like your good plans were messed up, you'll see that God had a far more beautiful plan. "Now we see things imperfectly as in a cloudy mirror, but then we will see everything with perfect clarity. All that I know now is partial and incomplete, but then I will know everything completely, just as God now knows me completely" (1 Corinthians 13:12).

Trust God, even with your unanswered questions and He will lead you into full recovery. Then, go help someone else discover the One who can heal them!

Discussion Questions

1. What doubts have you had about God or the Bible?

2. While God has not removed the possibility of doubt, what evidence do you see that helps you trust Him and trust what the Bible says about Him (that He is good, loving eternal, all-knowing, all-powerful)?

3. What does the writer of the book of Romans say about God? Why is this idea so important? Romans 11:33

4. What did Jesus promise to His followers? Based on this, how could you pray before reading the Bible? John 16:13, 14

5. How has the Bible helped you?

6. Paul, a man of God, prayed like this for his friends who had recently met God:

> *I pray that God, the glorious Father of our Lord Jesus, may give you wisdom and reveal Himself to you. That He will help you understand the great hope He is offering you—the hope of becoming His child and receiving an inheritance of immense wealth. I pray that you will understand that He has enormous power—more than enough to accomplish this for you. He showed His power when he raised Jesus from the dead and restored Him to His original position as co-Ruler over all other authorities and governments in the universe.*
> *~ Ephesians 1:16-23 (paraphrase)*

Which of the things he prayed for do you most feel you need? Why?

7. How does the writer of the book of Psalms describe God's Word? How does it help him? Psalm 119:97-105

STEP 13

Having had a spiritual experience as a result of these steps, we tried to carry this message to others and to practice these principles in all our affairs.

"Brothers, if someone is caught in a sin, you who are spiritual should restore him gently. But watch yourself, or you also may be tempted."

~ Galatians 6:1

CHAPTER 13

Laughing Out Loud With God

(Rejoicing in the Lord)

Invite others to join you in the great celebration with God.

God has rescued you, and He asks you to tell others what He's done for you. Jesus showed us His Father's heart and called us to share what we've seen with others. It is up to us to show other people that God desires to restore our sanity, and lead us into recovery.

"Just as you sent me into the world," said Jesus, "I am sending them into the world" (John 17:18); and "I am in them and you are in me...that the world will know that you sent me" (John 17:23). The apostle Paul said, "Clearly, you are a letter from Christ"; "Everyone can read it" (2 Corinthians 3:3, 2).

Letters and Lamps

In each one of His children, Jesus sends a letter to the world. If you follow Jesus, you are His letter to your family, your town, and the street where you live. Jesus is living in you and wants to speak through you to the hearts of those who don't know Him. Maybe they don't read the Bible or hear God's voice speaking to them from its pages. They don't recognize God's love through the world He made. But if you share what Jesus has done for you, perhaps others will come to understand His compassion. God may draw them close to Himself through you. He may win their hearts to love Him. Then they'll go and share Him, too.

You're like a lamp, lighting up the way to heaven. Jesus shines in you and you reflect His light to the world. Through your life and character, others will see Jesus and discover the joy of belonging to Him. You'll make the Christian life look as beautiful as it really is. But Christians who dwell on depressing thoughts and constantly complain give others a false picture of God and what it's like to follow Him. They give the idea that God doesn't want His children to be happy, which is a lie.

Roses and Thorns

Satan gloats when he can get you to distrust God and feel depressed. He enjoys your hopeless despair when you doubt that God is willing or able save you. He tries to make you feel that God's plans will bring you harm. Satan twists the truth and tries to make God look cold and harsh—as if He has no compassion for you. If he can get you to focus on those lies instead of what God is really like, he can cause you to stop trusting God and start rebelling against Him. Satan always tries to make God's way seem hard. He wants it to appear discouraging and difficult. If you complain about everything in your life, you'll be agreeing with Satan's lie that God doesn't care about you.

Many people go through life constantly thinking about their mistakes, failures, and disappointments. They are constantly overwhelmed and discouraged. It's like a person wandering off the path in a rose garden. Instead of enjoying the beauty and fragrance of the flowers, they get stuck on the thorns and cry and complain that the beautiful garden is not what they had hoped.

Have you had happy moments in your life? Has your heart ever been filled with joy in response to God's Spirit? When you look back on your life, do you see any good experiences? Don't you have God's promises right here with you, like fragrant flowers along the path? Let the beauty and sweetness of God's promises fill your heart with joy. The thorns will only hurt you and make you sad. If you always think about the tough times and complain about them to others, aren't you ignoring God's goodness and discouraging others from following Him?

It's not good to constantly think about all the painful memories of your past with all its sin and disappointment. It's not good to talk about them over and over until you're overwhelmed with discouragement. Discouraged souls are filled with darkness, shutting out God's light from their own lives and throwing a shadow on the lives of others.

Thank God for the bright pictures He presents to you. Collect the beautiful assurances of His love so you can review them over and over. Think about Jesus leaving His Father's throne and becoming a man so He could rescue us from Satan's power. Think of His triumph on the cross

which opened heaven to us. Think of the people you know
who He has rescued and healed. Think of His compassion
in helping them step into recovery and preparing them to
be with Him in heaven. These are the pictures God wants
us to focus on.

Never Speak Doubt

When we're suspicious of God's love and doubt His
promises, we dishonor Him and disappoint His Holy
Spirit. How would a mother feel if her children constantly
complained about her, saying that she didn't care about
their needs, when actually she had spent her whole life
trying help them? What if they doubted her love? It would
break her heart. How would any father feel to be treated
so badly by his children? And what does our heavenly Father think of us when we don't believe He loves us? It was
His love for us that led Him to give His only Son to save
our lives! The apostle Paul writes, "Since He did not spare
even His own Son but gave Him up for us all, won't He
also give us everything else?" (Romans 8:32). How many
people, by their actions, if not their words, are saying,
"God didn't do all this for me. Perhaps He loves others,
but He doesn't love me."

If you do this, it will hurt your own soul. Every word
of doubt you say or think invites Satan's temptations. It
makes you more inclined to doubt and causes the angels
who are watching over you to step back in sadness. When
Satan tempts you, don't speak any words of doubt or discouragement. If you choose to open the door to Satan's
suggestions, your mind will be filled with distrust and
rebellion. If you talk out loud about your negative feelings, every doubt you share not only strengthens your own
doubts, but sprouts like a bad weed in the lives of others.

It may be impossible to stop the effect of your words. Even if you recover from Satan's attack, others who have been discouraged by your influence may not be able to escape from the unbelief you have suggested. That's why it's so important to speak only words that will give spiritual strength and life!

Let your life and your words be focused on Jesus who is so eager to help everyone who struggles with sin. When you spend time with a friend, speak of what Jesus has done for you. As your friend becomes hungry for healing, your story will draw him to Jesus.

Everyone has problems. Everyone struggles with grief and sadness. Everyone has temptations that are hard to resist. Don't dump your problems on other people, but instead take everything to God. Make it a rule never to utter one word of doubt or discouragement. You can do a lot to encourage others and give them strength by your words of hope. Many people are bravely struggling with terrible temptation, nearly ready to give up in the battle with sin and the powers of evil. Make sure you don't discourage them. Help them to stay strong by speaking brave and hopeful words. Through your love, let them feel Jesus' love. "For we don't live for ourselves or die for ourselves" (Romans 14:7). Whether you realize it or not, your influence may encourage and strengthen others. Or it may discourage them and keep them away from Jesus.

Jesus' Example

Many people have a wrong idea about what Jesus was like. They think Jesus wasn't warm or cheerful, but that He was stern and harsh and cold. This false picture has alienated them against Jesus. Others see Jesus as a sad person who often wept and never smiled. It's true that Jesus was a "man of sorrows, and familiar with grief" because He opened His heart to everyone's pain and trouble (Isaiah 53). But despite the pain and hardship, He was full of joy. His face peaceful, not sad. Everywhere He went He brought a sense of rest and peace and happiness.

Jesus was deeply serious and intensely earnest, but He was never gloomy or depressed. If you're like Him, you'll have a strong sense of purpose and personal responsibility. You won't be frivolous or crude, but neither will you lose your joy. Following Jesus will give you deep peace. You'll learn to laugh out loud and enjoy being in your own skin. Like Jesus, your joy will come from helping others (Mark 10:45).

If you're always remembering the unkind and unfair actions of others, you'll find it impossible to love them as Jesus loves you. But if you think about the compassion Jesus has for you despite your mistakes, you'll have the same attitude toward others. Love and respect people, even when you can't help but see their faults and imperfections. Be humble, recognize your own weaknesses, and let that make you more patient and gentle with the faults of others. This will replace any selfishness in your heart with generosity and kindness.

Borrowing Trouble

David, the psalm writer said, "Trust in the Lord and do good. Then you will live safely in the land and prosper" (Psalm 37:3). Each day has plenty of problems, troubles, and frustrations, and we're all too ready to talk about them with others. We borrow trouble from the future, and indulge in our fears, and sound so stressed, that anyone might think God didn't care about us at all.

Some people are always afraid, worrying about potential problems, and getting upset over things that haven't even happened yet. And they do this, even though they are surrounded by the signs of God's love. Every day they enjoy His blessings, but they don't even seem to notice. Their minds continually focus on the fear of what could go wrong. Real problems, even little ones, completely blind them to the many things that have gone right. Their difficulties don't send them running to God, who could help them. Instead, their problems separate them from God because they can't stop worrying and complaining.

Why are we so ungrateful and distrustful? Jesus is our friend. All of heaven is interested in our happiness! Don't let difficulties and worries upset you. If we let our problems control us, there will always be something to frustrate and annoy us. Feeling sorry for yourself only wears you out—it won't help you get through your problems any better.

You may be troubled at work. Things may look very dark and you may be threatened with financial hardship. Don't be discouraged. "Give all your worries and cares to God, for He cares about you" (1 Peter 5:7). Stay calm and cheerful. Pray for wisdom to manage your responsibilities wisely to prevent losses and disaster. Do all you can on your part to bring about positive results. Jesus has promised His help, but He expects you also to make an effort. When you have relied upon your Helper and have done all you can, accept the results cheerfully.

God doesn't want His people to be weighed down with unnecessary cares. But He doesn't try to deceive us either. He doesn't say to us, "Don't be afraid, for there aren't any dangers in your path." God knows there are troubles and dangers, and He tells us so. He doesn't offer to take His people out of this world of sin and evil, but He provides them a safe refuge. His prayer for His disciples was,

"I'm not asking You to take them out of the world, but to keep them safe from the evil one" (John 17:15). "Here on earth," He says, "you will have many trials and sorrows. But take heart, because I have overcome the world" (John 16:33).

Lessons of Trust

Jesus taught His disciples valuable lessons about our need to trust in God. He planned these lessons to encourage His followers through all the ages, and they can still encourage and teach us today. Jesus pointed His followers to the birds that sing their songs of praise, untroubled with worries, for "they don't plant, or harvest" and yet the great Father provides for their needs. Jesus asks, "... aren't you far more valuable to Him than they are?" (Matthew 6:26). God, the great Provider, opens His hand and supplies all His creatures with what they need. He cares about the birds. He doesn't drop the food into their bills, but He takes care of their needs. They must gather the grains He has scattered for them. They must prepare the material for their little nests. They must feed their babies. But they sing as they work, for "your heavenly Father feeds them." And "aren't you far more valuable to Him than they are?" (Matthew 6:26). Aren't you, as His own children, more valuable than the birds? Won't the One who created us in His own image, who sustains our every breath, take care of our needs if we simply trust Him?

Jesus pointed to the flowers growing on the hillsides as an expression of God's love for us. "And why worry about your clothing?" Jesus asked. "Look at the lilies of the field and how they grow. They don't work or make their clothing" (Matthew 6:28). The beauty and simplicity of these natural flowers far surpasses the splendor of Solomon, one of the richest and wisest kings ever. The most beautiful clothes created by the most skilled designers can't compare with the natural grace and beauty of the flowers God created. Jesus asks, "And if God cares so wonderfully for wildflowers that are here today and thrown into the fire tomorrow, He will certainly care for you. Why do you have so little faith?" (Matthew 6:30). If God, the divine Artist, so carefully designs the delicate flowers that die after just a few days, how much greater care does He have for those who are created in His own image? The flowers remind us to stop worrying and trust Him.

God wants all His sons and daughters to be happy, peaceful, and obedient. Jesus says, "I am leaving you with a gift—peace of mind and heart. And the peace I give is a gift the world cannot give. So don't be troubled or afraid" (John 14:27); "I have told you these things so that you will be filled with my joy. Yes, your joy will overflow!" (John 15:11).

Looking Ahead With Joy

If you look for happiness outside of God's good ways, the happiness you find won't satisfy you and it won't last. When it's gone, all you'll have left is loneliness, pain, and grief. But in God's ways, you'll find real joy and satisfaction. God doesn't leave you to wander around with no map and live a life filled with regret and disappointment. Even if you suffer in this life, you can still have joy looking forward to the life beyond.

But even here on earth you can have the joy of a close friendship with Jesus. You can have His love and the comfort of His presence right now. Everything that happens in your life can bring you closer to Him and nearer to heaven—the peaceful home you'll share with Him some-day. Don't stop trusting Him. Keep saying, "Up to this point the Lord has helped us!" (1 Samuel 7:12), and He will help us to the end. Look at all God has done for His people in the past, and remember how Jesus has rescued you from being destroyed by Satan. Think about His kind-ness—the tears He's wiped away, the pain He's soothed, the worries He's removed, the fears He's chased away, the needs He's provided, the good things He's given—and let these encourage and strengthen your for the rest of your journey here on Earth.

There will certainly be new problems and hard days in the future, especially in the last great trouble soon to come on this earth. But you can look back on the past, as you also look ahead to the future, and say, "Up to this point the Lord has helped us!" (1 Samuel 7:12); and "... May you be secure all your days" (Deuteronomy 33:25). Your problems won't be greater than the strength God will give you to endure them. So take up your work wher-ever you find it, trusting that whatever may come your way, God will give you the strength you need. And after a little while, heaven's gates will be thrown open to wel-come God's children. Then from the lips of Jesus, the King of glory, the invitation will sound to their ears like the most beautiful music, "Come, you who are blessed by my Father, inherit the Kingdom prepared for you from the creation of the world" (Matthew 25:34).

Jesus will welcome every person He has rescued into the home He has prepared for them. Their friends won't be the evil people of the earth: liars, idolaters, the im-pure, and unbelieving. Instead, their friends will be those who have overcome Satan, and through God's grace, have formed perfect characters. God has removed every defect and given them a character like Jesus' own beautiful character. As they enter their new home, He will give them His glory, far brighter than the sun, reflecting the holiness in their hearts. They will stand before God's great white throne without shame, and they will be as honored and privileged as any angel.

Think of this inheritance God has planned for you, His beloved child. Is "anything worth more than your soul?" (Matthew 16:26). You may be poor now, but you have within you a wealth and honor the world can never give. Rescued and cleansed from sin, with all your noble powers dedicated to the service of God, you are valued in heaven as if you were the only one Jesus died to save. God and the holy angels will hold a celebration when you walk into heaven and will sing songs of joy and victory over you!

How cool is that!

Discussion Questions

1. If you, as a follower of Jesus, are a letter from God to your friends and family, what message are they getting?

2. When life is hard, why do we complain? What is the result?

3. If saying an idea strengthens that idea, what ideas are becoming strongest in your mind? How can you change that? Philippians 4:8

4. What are some of the best things God has shown you or done for you?

5. The Bible says that Jesus was a man of sorrows and familiar with grief (Isaiah 53:3). How could He then give us peace and joy? John 14:27; John 15:11

6. When life gets tough, what can you do? 1 Peter 5:7, John 14:1, Psalm 28:7

7. God has not promised that life will be easy. But what has He promised? Hebrews 13:5; Matthew 28:20 John 14:1-3

   Tell about a time when that promise really helped you.

Answer Guide for Discussion Questions

Chapter 1

5. Adam and Eve were created in the image of God. When the archangel, Lucifer (now known as Satan—see Luke 10:18), rebelled against God he was cast out of heaven. He came to earth and deceived Adam and Eve and rebellion against God went viral. As a result, they unleashed a tide of evil that affected not only themselves but all creation. Rebellion against God became part of the DNA of all humans. Instead of being God's children, having a character like His, we are warped and twisted by the disease of sin.

6. God spoke to men directly and in dreams (like Abraham and Samuel). He gave them messages for the people and told them to write them down for all who would come after to read (like David and Jeremiah). God's ultimate revelation of His love was Jesus who He sent to show us, in human form, that He's crazy about us and delights in our healing.

Chapter 2

1. It is not enough just to know God loves us because we live under a death penalty. Without intervention, we are doomed to die. We need more than love, we need a God who loves us enough to rescue us from the sin that enslaves us and from eternal death.

3. Allowing sin, with all the misery it causes, to continue forever would be the worst kind of cruelty. You could call it hell. God does not want us to just exist forever, continuing in eternal misery and grief. He wants us to really <u>live</u> forever—to celebrate life. That's why God is executing a plan to eliminate sin completely.

4. There is only one Person in the universe who is able to remove our sin-infected heart and give us a new clean one. Only One who could take our infection on Himself and die the death we were doomed to die. Only One who could give us eternal life <u>without</u> sin. That person is Jesus.

Chapter 3

1. God is working to reconcile the world—every person—to Himself. No one, not even the worst of us, is excluded from His effort to reconcile us. God called David, the murderer. He called Paul, who had tortured and killed Christians. He calls all whose sins are so intense. And He assures even the worst of us that He sent Jesus, not to condemn us, but to save us.

2. It is a lie to think that you are not a mess. Jesus urges you to ask Him for the "eye salve" of the Holy Spirit to open your eyes so you can see and remove the delusion that you are fine as you are. The Spirit will show you not only the harm you have done, but also the glory and holiness of Jesus, who takes away your sin. The story of Jesus giving sight to the blind man who came to Him illustrates what He wants to do for your spiritual blindness.

4. We can't fix ourselves or any of the damage we have done any more than a leopard can get rid of his spots. If we wait until we make things right, we will wait forever. Only God can change us. We have to go to God as we are.

Chapter 4

1. God does not force us to confess. Instead He helps us to see the full extent of our sin. He draws us to Himself as the only One who can address the deep heart-longing that drove us to sin in the first place. A forced confession omits such repentance, so it is of no value.

4. True confession is specific. It does not make excuses or try to hide. Anyone who truly confesses wants desperately to be forgiven and to have the sin removed from their heart so they can be close to God.

5. If we have harmed someone else, we may need to confess to them as well. Every person belongs to God and He does not want us to hurt them. When you hurt someone, God asks you to confess to them. Note that there are some cases where confessing to someone will actually cause more harm. If you aren't sure, it may help to seek counsel from a Godly mentor before making such a confession.

6. God promises to forgive you and to cleanse all the sin from your heart. His goal isn't just to soothe your fears by forgiving you. His goal is to restore you to be like Him as in the original creation—to make you clean and good like He is.

Chapter 5

1. Sin has made us the living dead. We are sick and brutally wounded. We are captive slaves of the devil and our own addictions.

2. God won't force us to change. Only as we submit to Him can He heal us so we can celebrate life.

3. Jesus said it is not possible to be only half His.

4. God asks you to give up only those things that do not satisfy the hunger and thirst of your soul. His great loving heart longs to forgive you and to provide the best of everything that will feed your soul.

6. Surrender begins with a choice. While we cannot change our will, we can choose to give our will to God. We can ask Him to show us what is in our hearts and lead us in His good ways. He will work in us to change our will, our desires, and our hearts

Chapter 6

2. Jesus proved that He has the authority to forgive sin and heal a sick soul when He did the far easier task of healing sick bodies.

3. God promises if you ask anything according to His will, He will give it to you. Jesus said it is the will of the Father to save you. God says He takes no pleasure in the death of the wicked and urges you to repent so you won't die. Therefore, you can be sure that if you ask forgiveness, He will forgive you.

4. God assures you that if you confess your sins, He will forgive you and remove all sin from you—even the worst of sins. He says He will freely forgive you and will totally block your sin from view. And He says that once He has done that, you are no longer condemned. He delights to save you and rejoices over you.

5. The father waited eagerly to forgive his runaway son as soon as he caught a glimpse of him. God does even more than that. He speaks to your heart while you are still lost in your junk, showing you that He loves you and longs to forgive you and heal you and bring you close to Himself.

Chapter 7

1. Jesus' followers do what He commands. They do the will of the Father just as He did. The will of the Father is that they love each other.

3. Jesus described His followers as a lamp or a candle set out to provide light in a dark place so all may see.

4. We must look to Jesus to rescue us. He forgives us and He gives us His Spirit to join with us and help us. As we follow the Spirit's lead, revealed to us in God's Word and in our minds, our desires and actions will change.

Chapter 8

1. The Bible frequently compares spiritual growth to a seed that grows into a mature plant and produces a harvest.

2. The seed does not begin living on its own. Life come from God. The seed does not grow on its own. A seed grows when it is exposed to sunlight and water. Its role is to take in what is provided to it.

3. Jesus is the Light of the World, the Living Water, the Bread of Life. Only He can provide what we need for spiritual growth.

4. Your role is to remain in Jesus.

5. You will remain in Jesus when you accept His love, obey His directions, keep looking to Him and His example, go to Him in prayer every morning, seek His guidance and trust Him, commit your plans to Him, believe Him, and come to Him for rest and to learn from Him.

Chapter 9

1. Healthy plants produce good fruit.

2. Jesus' followers will remain in Him and produce much fruit. Unless they remain in Him they can't produce any fruit.

3. All of us produce bad fruit naturally—we damage ourselves and each other.

4. Love, joy, peace, patience, kindness, goodness, faith, gentleness, self-control, righteousness, truth.

5. Growth is a gradual process. It begins very small, and it doesn't happen all at once. But as you grow, you will produce fruit— you will help others find the healing and safety you have found in Jesus.

Chapter 10

2. God loves us faithfully.

3. Ask for the Spirit to guide you. Search the scriptures daily. Encourage each other daily. Find a quiet place to be alone with God each day. Ask God to teach you.

4. If you have seen Me, you have see the Father.

5. Jesus says to you: I have loved you with an everlasting love. Though your sins are the worst, I will cleanse you. My plans are to give you hope, not to harm you. Despite all your past, I will heal you and comfort you. I will satisfy all the hunger and thirst of your heart. I will never send you away. The Father sent me to bring you home. I'm preparing a place for you, and I will come back for you so we can be together forever.

Chapter 11

1. God the Father knows your needs before you ask Him. Before you call He will answer you. Anything you ask in Jesus' name He will give you. He is able to do far beyond what you can ask or imagine.

2. Reasons to pray:

   a. If you seek God with all your heart, you will find Him.

   b. If you ask Him to help you believe, He will.

   c. If you confess, He will forgive and cleanse you.

   d. If you ask Him for wisdom, He will give it to you.

   e. If you submit to God and resist the Devil you will escape evil.

   f. If you think about God in everything you do, He can guide you.

   g. If you are hungry for Him, He can fill you.

   h. If you go to God, He can heal your brokenness.

   i. If you seek refuge in His strength, He will protect you.

   j. If you come to Him, believing in Him, He will give you joy, peace, and hope.

Chapter 12

3. That God's wisdom and His ways are unknowable. If we could comprehend all that God is, He would hardly be worthy of our worship. We couldn't trust Him with the problems that are bigger than we are. Eternity would be a frightening uncertainty without an infinite and infinitely wise God.

4. Jesus promised the Spirit will teach us. We can ask Him for understanding before we open the Bible.

7. He loves it and meditates on it daily. It gives him exceptional wisdom and understanding. It keeps him from evil because God teaches him. It is sweet to him. It is like a light to help him see the way.